PRAISE FOR TEDDY RILEY

"I was very young and did not know Teddy as a producer until he got in town, and then I started to realize all the things that he had done in the past. Everything from all the Kool Moe Dee music to the very first thing I ever heard him do, which was a song called 'The Show' with Doug E. Fresh and Slick Rick. Teddy's production influenced early hip-hop like beyond, and his R&B was just as crazy as well. New Jack Swing is one of the most timeless sounds that on the surface, still to this day, if you play 'Remember the Time' by Michael Jackson, it still rings, but man, you can play Guy's 'Groove Me' right behind that, and it would sound just as timeless and amazing. His work with Guy was unmatched, but do yourself a favor: If you haven't listened to 'The Show' with Doug E. Fresh and Slick Rick, it will change your life. You realize this guy was the first to use the shaker and make it the way that he did; he's just still the dope and will always be.

"Growing up so near to Future Studios in Virginia Beach, the way Chad Hugo and I looked at it, we'd heard there was this producer that was there, but never knew that the studio was right next door to the other side of this little bridge connected to my high school. By then, as a producer, Teddy had already done *Dangerous* by Michael Jackson, and it was crazy knowing he was right over there. We used to see the Ferraris and the Range Rovers and the Mercedes 500 Benz pulling in all the time, and that was just inspiring as a kid. My first time meeting Teddy wasn't at a high school talent show; we were washing cars and had a manager who was very tight with Teddy, and always promised he would introduce us to him, but he needed help getting the cars cleaned. One day, Teddy was walking in the studio, and the car wash owner had gone to him and said, 'Teddy, you really need to meet these guys,' and he was like, 'Okay cool, come up here at 11 o'clock tonight.' I thought, *Man, that's crazy, but this is the way that we work.* So when we got there, he introduced himself and said, 'I heard that you rap? I want you to write this rap for me,' and that's when he played me 'Rump Shaker,' and I wrote his verse that night.

"From working with him, I also learned how Teddy blended so many different sounds together. He's just such an incredible mixologist of so many different styles, from church to speeding up Go-Go rhythms, making the cocktail that became New Jack Swing. And seeing and hearing his ability to record vocals, the vocal treatments pretty much changed the way people listen to music still to this day. He was amazing with the vocoder for himself as well, but he was a great vocal producer. He was also an all-around really brilliantly gifted musician, and people don't know this, but the reason K-Pop sounds like it does is because he was there, holding class. He informed a lot of the K-Pop producers and their form of music. That's why when you go to Asia, still to this day, a lot of the chord changes on so many of the songs have very R&B changes. That was because of Teddy Riley."

—Pharrell Williams

"Hip-hop and R&B had never really been put together the way we put it together. I think we were the first that basically did that: mixed the two genres the way we took rap beats and made R&B songs out of them. That was what they called 'New Jack Swing.'"

—Bobby Brown

"I call Teddy my little brother. I mean, even when we argue, it's like brothers. We have that bond like brothers and sisters have, and even though we're not blood-related, nobody can tell me that's not my little brother right there. It made me feel good to be able to introduce the world to what he had to offer. It makes me feel good that I was one of many that he started with, that the world embraced us musically, and that we have the legacy that we have today. If you name all the artists that mattered during the '80s, '90s, and early 2000s, Teddy musically had a lot to do with it. He's got to be one of the top ten hip-hop/R&B producers of all time, so he'll definitely go down as one of the pioneers of music, because if his name is not mentioned, something's wrong."

—Keith Sweat

"What Teddy Riley did was create a whole different sound for R&B that kind of puts you in the mind of Chuck Brown, who came from playing with salsa bands and used a lot of percussion and decided to bring those percussions into R&B and merge the two—R&B with salsa—and ended up creating Go-Go. I feel like Teddy pretty much did the same thing. I know that he comes from a gospel background, but a lot of the bouncy chords he uses were really unique, and he created his own lane, just like Chuck Brown did. So, Teddy's definitely one of the greatest producers in my book: He has a unique style that I've watched many try to duplicate, but none could ever really emulate. Teddy paved the way for a lot of new artists to be showcased, and to resurrect careers of fading artists."

—Big Daddy Kane

"Teddy's just dope. I love to hear another producer do a bomb record that has nothing to do with the sound that I've been using, because I hear a lot of songs out there right now where people are using the sounds that I was using on *The Chronic* album and Snoop's album, and it's whack to me! I like to hear something that's like, *Damn, why didn't I think of that?* That's what I like to hear."

—Dr. Dre

"Before I was making records, I was buying [Teddy's] records. I was inspired by the whole movement that he had with the New Jack Swing and the R&B records from Al B. Sure! and Keith Sweat. He's a guy that you sit back and wait for his records to come out, so you can see what you're going to do next."

—Snoop Dogg

"In my opinion—and I might be biased—I think Teddy is probably the most underrated great producer of all time. Quincy Jones goes down the way he goes down because of Michael Jackson, even though he's done tons of work outside of Michael Jackson. But because of *Thriller*, he's the first name when you say, 'Greatest Producer.' You can't say that without saying Quincy Jones, but Teddy wasn't just a hip-hop producer and he wasn't just an R&B producer, and very few producers are both. You're either doing one or the other, so Teddy, again, is for my money, pound for pound, one of the best, because it's very hard to shift from both sides. So, I think he's literally the all-time underrated great."

—Kool Moe Dee

"For me, Teddy has always been incredible. He's always been an incredible writer, an incredible producer, and one that has his own sound from the get-go, going back to the early days, when he worked on 'The Show' by Doug E. Fresh, to Michael Jackson and all the other things he's done. Teddy no question is one of the people and producers and writers I most respect, and when I look at what I've done, and what me and L.A. did, I feel as though, as a writer, I was always just figuring out how to stay in the game and write things that felt good, but I never felt like a pioneer, so to say. I just kind of felt like I was doing what I did, maybe pioneering love songs to a certain extent, but I felt like Teddy was a pioneer. He's been as much of an inspiration to me as he may say I was to him."

—Babyface

"There's a lot of young producers that came from under my wing, just the same way I came from under Teddy's, who are having tremendous success now. Teddy Riley is a genre alone. He created New Jack Swing, there's no other way to put it, and New Jack Swing was its own genre. You couldn't categorize it as R&B or pop or hip-hop; it was all combined."

—Rodney Jerkins

"That's who I patterned myself after because Teddy is not just a hip-hop producer. That's how I try to approach music. Teddy is a producer who can *also* do hip-hop. You're talking about a person who produced Guy and did Doug E. Fresh's 'The Show.' Hello? Teddy Riley did 'The Show'! If there wasn't a Teddy Riley, there would be no Timbaland, no Neptunes, or me."

—will.i.am

"If it was a beautiful, sunny day outside and you got brand-new sneakers or a brand-new outfit, when you walk outside, everybody's going to stare at you good. That's how it felt being back on stage together with Teddy, just us vibing with each other. One thing I know is that when we do 'Piece of My Love,' we've got the audience, and from there on, we have them."

—Aaron Hall

"To understand Riley's impact, you have to meticulously connect the dots to a long list of producers and artists who have worshipped at the altar of the genius one-man-band. Without the Guy and Blackstreet leader's blueprint, there would be no Mary J. Blige, Jermaine Dupri, Jodeci, Usher, Timbaland, Missy Elliott, Dru Hill, the Neptunes, Chris Brown, The-Dream, or Bruno Mars. He was merging rap and soul before Roddy Ricch was literally conceived."

—*VIBE*, 2018

Remember the Times

A Memoir

Teddy Riley

with Jake Brown

Gallery Books / 13A
New York Amsterdam/Antwerp London
Toronto Sydney/Melbourne New Delhi

GALLERY BOOKS/13A
An Imprint of Simon & Schuster, LLC
1230 Avenue of the Americas
New York, NY 10020

All photos courtesy of the author.

First 13A/Gallery Books hardcover edition February 2026

13A is a trademark of Charles Suitt and is used with permission.

GALLERY BOOKS and colophon are registered trademarks of Simon & Schuster, LLC

Simon & Schuster strongly believes in freedom of expression and stands against censorship in all its forms. For more information, visit BooksBelong.com.

For information about special discounts for bulk purchases, please contact Simon & Schuster Special Sales at 1-866-506-1949 or business@simonandschuster.com.

The Simon & Schuster Speakers Bureau can bring authors to your live event. For more information or to book an event, contact the Simon & Schuster Speakers Bureau at 1-866-248-3049 or visit our website at www.simonspeakers.com.

Interior design by Jason Snyder

Manufactured in the United States of America

10 9 8 7 6 5 4 3 2 1

Library of Congress Control Number: 2025934894

ISBN 978-1-6680-5645-5
ISBN 978-1-6680-5647-9 (ebook)

 Let's stay in touch! Scan here to get book recommendations, exclusive offers, and more delivered to your inbox.

I dedicate this book to my mother, Mildred Riley;
Gene Griffin; my sister, Nece; and Uncle Willie Brewington.

Contents

Foreword

BARRY MICHAEL COOPER
Screenwriter, New Jack City

New Jack Swing is the musical phoenix that rose from the ashes of the crack epidemic—Teddy Riley's orchestration of life during wartime, set to a swing beat . . .

I grew up in Harlem in the Esplanade Gardens; he grew up just a few blocks away in the St. Nicholas projects. I respected and loved Teddy's music so much from the first time I heard it. I was working at the *Village Voice* as a music critic and I started hearing about this kid making music at the Rooftop, this roller disco that was like the Studio 54 for gangsters. Alpo, Rich Porter, Azie Faison, Kevin Chiles, all those legendary street guys hung out there, and Teddy was making tapes there. He was fifteen years old at the time, and I remember people coming back to tell me, "Barry, have you heard about this kid Teddy Riley?"

I asked, "Who's Teddy Riley?" And they would give me the tapes back that he was making. I'd listen, and at first I said, "This is not a teenager making this kind of music—that's bullshit. So, who's really doing it?"

Teddy and his music created a paradigmatic shift in the '80s and a lot of people don't really give him credit for that. He was in the right place at the right time. Had there not been a crack epidemic, I'm not saying Teddy Riley would not have happened, but the profundity and the power of his music would have been different. It's like he got the assignment: I'm growing up among killers, murders, and this drug that's absolutely suffocating the life out of my community, so let me create a soundtrack that explores that crisis, exposes it, defines it, and hopefully will offer a way of escape.

What Teddy was doing musically is what I was doing on the page, and that parallel is why we connected so personally. I was trying to tell stories about the hood with some kind of classicism. I had written a story for the *Village Voice* in December 1987 titled "New Jack City Eats Its Young." So, when I wrote a story on Teddy in October 1988, I called what he was doing "New Jack Swing." I remember rereading *The Great Gatsby*. I was thinking about how Fitzgerald called the 1920s "the hour of profound human change," then I realized, *That's what Teddy is doing. That's exactly what he's doing. He doesn't even realize it, because it's organic to him.* He was taking in all of this from the streets, the kids from St. Nicholas, the gangsters who protected him, the Rooftop, and then he added another element that I don't even think he's aware of, almost a classical influence—Richard Wagner or Beethoven. He was taking all these musical elements, melding them, and making them almost otherworldly.

Then, when I found out this dude was recording hits in his mom's house in the St. Nicholas projects, I said to myself, "That makes him even more of a genius. This guy is part of the elite. He's a bridge that connects Prince, Marvin Gaye, Barry White, Michael Jackson, P-Funk, to the '80s."

Guys like Gusto and all of those local Harlem gangsters who looked out for him back then, they knew that Teddy was a prodigy. They may not have contextualized it that way, but they knew that this kid was special; it was, "Hands off! You don't mess with him." Because amid all the horror that crack inflicted on the Black community, and specifically Harlem, Teddy represented hope. In the back of those guys' minds, whether it was conscious or not, they thought, *He's going to be the seed that will grow positively. He represents the potential of greatness coming out of this community. People think all Black men are selling drugs and killing each other, but not this guy. This guy has a gift that's going to change the world.* And guess what? He did. New Jack Swing and what Teddy was doing, and what Teddy continued to do, changed the world.

I still remember the exact moment when I asked him, "Do you realize what you're doing?" and he genuinely didn't. So, then I asked, "What are you going to call this? What do you call this music?" And when he replied, "I don't know," that's when I said, "Let me give you a suggestion: Quincy Jones, George Jackson, and Warner Bros. just hired me to write a movie called *New Jack City*. I think you should call this music New Jack Swing." I then went to my editors at the *Village Voice* and told them, "You've got to call the story 'Teddy Riley's New Jack Swing,' because this music is so different."

By the time we got to "My Prerogative" in 1988, with everything he and Aaron Hall did for Bobby Brown, it was over! That's the record where label executives began saying, "If you don't have the Teddy Riley sound, we don't want to hear it!" I heard that it was Eddie Murphy who advised Quincy Jones, "You need to check Teddy out for Michael Jackson." This was when they were recording *Dangerous*, and I'm going to tell you something: On "Remember the Time" and "In the Closet," Teddy just went off. It's like he faced working with the greatest pop star in the world and still said to himself, "I'm going to take you to another level." That's what he did with "Remember the Time." If you listen to that track today, to me, it still sounds futuristic. It's both of its time and of another time—and again that's genius. You cannot teach it. Like I said, there are plenty of other genius producers and songwriters who preceded Teddy, but none of their records sounded like what Teddy was doing.

Teddy's music is all I was listening to while I was writing *New Jack City*, to the point where I remember driving through Laurel Canyon with the late great George Jackson, one of the film's producers, listening to a song he'd produced for Kingpin, and I said, "You know Teddy has to have music in this movie! He's from Harlem— he's Harlem's Beethoven, or Mozart, even. There's no way of doing this without his music involved." And he replied, "Absolutely right, Barry." It turned out that Teddy's music was all George was listening to, too, and Teddy wound up doing the title track "New Jack City" with Guy. It was almost like a commercial for New Jack Swing.

As I was writing the movie, I was listening to Keith Sweat, Guy, *New Generation* by the Classical Two—all of Teddy's records on perpetual repeat. That powered me. I was feeling it, like "Okay Teddy, come on, bring it, bring it. We're from Harlem. We know all the killers. We know all the scramblers. We know all the drug dealers. We know all of that—help me bring it to this page." And that's what he did. Listening to his music inspired me.

That music still resonates to this day, over thirty years later. We're on the other side of the millennium now, and yet it is more powerful than ever. Whatever we hear today, no matter the tempo, is rooted in Teddy's innovations. He was a precursor and mentor to Timbaland, to Pharrell, to Missy, and to all these artists who he taught how to rethink R&B. We're living in a machine world, we're the ghosts in the machine, and our music should reflect that. But Teddy was the pivot of change in the music industry, and it wasn't just music. It was a movement.

It was also a beautiful time. From Harlem to the farmlands of Idaho to Los Angeles, from Portland, Maine to Portland, Oregon, from the UK to France, to Asia and Africa, the movement became global. It created careers for people, and so much of that is rooted in the music of Teddy Riley, because if there was any other music to accompany that film, it wouldn't have worked as well as it did. Teddy was a game changer.

CHAPTER ONE

St. Nicholas

*"I knew he was going to be a star one day. Every
mother says that about their child, but you could
just always feel the talent in Teddy growing."*

—MILDRED RILEY, MY MOM

was just five years old the first time I ever got up before a big crowd.
My babysitter had taken me to the Apollo Theater for the first time
to see a Gladys Knight concert, and while she was singing "Neither
One of Us (Wants to Be the First to Say Goodbye)"—and it must have
been fate, because we were sitting in the front row—Gladys actually
had a stagehand pick me up and put me on the stage with her! I remember I was dancing around and the crowd went wild, and that was the
first time I said to myself, "I want to be a star." Hearing the way that
audience lit up for me, I knew that I wanted to be on that stage.

When I was a young kid, I was not popular. I didn't really stand
out until I started playing music. Growing up in the heart of Harlem

in the St. Nicholas housing projects wasn't all bad like you see in the movies: There was hide-and-go-seek, freeze tag, hotcakes and butter, water fights in the summertime where we'd spray the fire hydrant at each other before the police would come around and make us turn it off. We played in baseball and basketball tournaments on the local courts, and in fact, my partners from growing up back then later started the Rutgers University Basketball Tournaments on 40th Street and Rucker Park on West 155th Street, which have since become so locally storied that films have been made about them.

That was the bright side of growing up in the inner city. Then there was the dark side, where people would get shot and killed in front of my building, or even in my hallway. I remember once a friend of the family got kidnapped and held hostage by a guy who lived in my building. The kidnapper had a standoff with the NYPD and shot two cops—and this is a man who you'd never suspect would do anything like that. So, you never knew what to expect, and while it was safe inside my apartment, outside you'd hear and sometimes see gunshots. It was happiness, sadness, excitement, heartfelt moments, and tragedy all wrapped up in one existence.

I would wake up every morning and say to God, "Bless my mother, my sister, Joyce, and my brother, Markell," because we never knew what we'd be walking out into that day, living in the projects. Some days it was all sunshine, but other days you could feel the danger in the air. That's part of why my brother and I growing up never wanted to sleep apart—we always had each other's backs. In fact, the only person in my family I've never had an argument or fight with is my brother, who is four years my junior. But my whole family has always been close. Even though today we don't speak all the time, when we do, it's like we've never left one another's side. My family were also my first and biggest fans. I would put on little talent shows for them in the living room when I was four or five years old, performing other people's songs before I'd started writing my own. Around that same age, I picked up my first ever instrument: my uncle Leroy's guitar. He was always over at our house, and I would watch him play. When he set it down, I'd pick it up and try to imitate what I'd seen and heard him do. He would play B.B. King or Jimmy Reed or something from the church, and I would follow him by ear.

As music continued to consume me, my mom's family and my godmother were always going on about how I would be a star one day. My mother never pushed me like that, not when I was young. I think she wanted to allow me to just be a kid, if that's what I wanted. But as I turned six, seven, eight, music kept pulling me deeper and deeper. And when I turned nine, I'll never forget my mother's voice becoming louder in my squad of cheerleaders, because she could see I was beginning to show something special musically. That's when she began pushing me to play piano and organ in Little Flower Baptist Church.

That was a big deal, as you can imagine, because it expanded the audience of people who I would be performing for, and that in turn became a huge influence on me because it helped me develop as a performer. The keyboard player in our church, who couldn't play very well, left abruptly, so all of a sudden they didn't have a pianist—and then this little nine-year-old kid steps into those shoes. I'll never forget the first time. We were sitting in the pew one Sunday morning, there was no one at the keyboard, and my mother said to me, "You get up there and play," and I did because I was told to do it by my mother! That experience taught me how to not be shy, and it felt really good, too, because people seemed to like listening to me—the first time anyone outside my immediate family had heard me play, which also helped me gain confidence as a developing musician and performer.

After that, I started attending Universal Temple, where I was the *only* piano player. Still, I felt like I wasn't learning what I needed to know, because I was playing while everybody was singing. But we went to this church anniversary celebration one weekend, where there were singers and musicians from different churches. I was there playing piano for my church, but then this other church's musicians came up, and they had a drummer, and I said, "You know what, I need to find a church like that closer to my church!" At Universal Temple, where Jazzy Jay from Afrika Bambaataa's crew was the *drummer*, and their DJ Red Alert was the DJ for the church!

You couldn't ask to have anything more than the DJ and drummer for Afrika Bambaataa. The preacher was the organist until my idol and the best organist I've ever worked with, Andre, replaced him. He was the lead music director for the church band. He showed me lots on piano, including playing church chords. That's when I knew that the piano would be my main instrument and inspiration.

◆ ◆ ◆ ◆ ◆

I got my first synthesizer at age ten. It was a fun time because my little brother was five and six when I was nine and ten, and he used to break-dance along to my music when I played in our bedroom. It felt good to see him get that excited by what I was doing, and that feeling only grew when I performed my first "real" concert in grade school with my music teacher, Mr. Cornelius. I was performing with the choir at a school Christmas assembly, and at the end of the assembly, he gave me a solo spot singing "All I Want for Christmas."

I remember feeling terror and exhilaration all at once, but I pulled off the song and got nice applause from the crowd along with the rest of my classmates. Well, that reaction inspired me to take my solo spot a step further. I don't know quite what came over me, but the next thing I knew, I had jumped up behind a drum kit they had set up on stage, and I started banging away in front of the crowd.

I mean, I wore those drums *out*, and that was the moment where the girls my age suddenly knew what I could do and started paying me attention, which was a big deal for me because prior to that, I was always known as the shy kid in class. I had a crush back then on a beautiful girl in my class named Dana, and I'd been so clueless around her that I even put Vaseline all over my face and came to school like that, trying to impress her! Naturally that backfired because her response to me when I'd worked up the nerve to say hi was, "Why is your face so greasy?" My crush had crushed me, but once my personality lit up on that stage, that whole dynamic changed. I started to gain some popularity among the girls in my class as word of my musical talent started getting around the neighborhood.

I attended Harriet Tubman PS 154 elementary school in Harlem from pre-K all the way through the fifth grade. Year in, year out, we had lunchtime in the same schoolyard, which happened to face the back parking lot of the Apollo Theater. I felt like I was getting two educations, because it seemed like every time we would be playing out there, I'd see people coming in and out of this building, loading musical instruments and gear in and out. I didn't know exactly what was going on, but I remember being instantly mesmerized because of my fascination with music.

The big "aha!" moment came one day when I recognized James Brown among those people walking in and out of the Apollo. You can't forget that hair and the tight jumpsuits he would wear, or if it was winter, the fancy fur jackets. Then I started recognizing other faces I'd seen on TV: guys like Johnnie Taylor and B.B. King, who I knew distinctly even at that young age. Then one day we saw The Temptations, who all dressed alike. My brother, Markell, remembers seeing Parliament-Funkadelic pull up—the spaceship was parked outside and everything.

After that, it became a hobby for me and my friends at lunch and after school every day to sit across the street from that parking lot and people-watch, trying to see who could recognize stars first. Though it was kind of a game between us, at the same time, I'd started dreaming of becoming a star myself. I remember my friends would talk about wanting to become a hustler, or a fireman, or an astronaut when they grew up, but I always said I wanted to be a star. Though it probably seemed a million miles away at the time, seeing all this music business behind-the-scenes activity right there in front of me, day in and day out, only fueled that dream.

Our lunchtime was during the theater's usual sound check, so we'd see all these famous R&B groups and soul singers come outside in their stage clothes while it was still daylight, maybe to have a smoke or just to get a bit of fresh air before they went on stage. That made a *huge* impression on me as a kid, soaking all that up. It made these stars seem not so far away, and allowed me to see them off stage as real people like myself—especially on those lucky occasions when we actually got to meet some of them.

That was easier after school, and a bunch of us neighborhood kids would always go up to 126th Street and wait around to see who came out or pulled up to load in for that night's show. An important date for me came on the day they were preparing to put on a Motown concert featuring a bunch of their biggest acts of the later 1970s. It was dazzling to my young eyes: There were TV cameras everywhere, and I actually got up the courage to sneak inside the backstage door for the first time, determined to meet The Temptations and the Jackson 5.

Meeting the Jacksons was an especially big deal for me, having watched their cartoon as a little kid and their live television performances too. I remember shaking Jackie's hand first, then Jermaine's, then Marlon's, then Tito's, but I was kind of bummed out because I didn't get to meet Michael (that day). Back then, he was always kept separate from the other brothers by his dad, Joe. But meeting the other Jacksons was still a very big deal for me because I wanted to be one of them, up onstage dancing and singing, entertaining people, getting that same reaction out of the crowd I had when I was five and got put up on stage with Gladys Knight. It was infectious and made me work on developing my own musical talents with that much more focus.

Back then, my bedroom was a small room about half the size of my studio now, like ten feet by ten feet, and me and my brother shared it. We had a bunk bed, and we shared a dresser. Right next to our dresser was a radiator, which we utilized to heat up our candy, our Now and Laters, so that came in handy. We had posters on the wall of Batman and Robin and Superman—we couldn't afford the toys, so we made do with the posters. My brother and I also loved collecting all the local concert bills that would paper the subway station walls advertising Battles in the Park with all the hottest New York DJs. This gave early fuel to my dream of one day making it onto the same stages. (Many of the hottest emcees who got on those mics each weekend I would later make records with—who knew?)

CHAPTER TWO

Total Climax

"I always told him when he was young,
'God gave you a gift; use it.'"

—MILDRED RILEY

W hen I was twelve years old, in 1980, I got my first keyboard. It was a Casio CZ-10, and it was like my best friend because I never rolled anywhere without it: school, the street, everywhere. Across the street from my projects, I went to Universal Temple church all throughout my childhood until I was fourteen. It was a great training experience, from playing keyboards in the church band to just about every other instrument. But as I entered my teens, I was ready for a *bigger* challenge musically, and boy did I know how to pick one.

I was actually walking up Seventh Avenue headed up to 125th Street on my way to the barbershop when I heard a band rehearsing.

The funny thing is I used to see and hear the band Total Climax practicing every day in the basement of a building across the street from my projects. I quickly became their biggest fan and began showing up to their practices every day to watch and listen. This went on for five or six months until I decided I *needed to be* in that band. One day I gathered up enough heart to take my little Casio over there and announce, "I play piano."

Naturally, they didn't believe me and said, "Shorty, you don't play. Get out of here." I went home disappointed. I was determined, though, so I gathered up my courage and came back again the next week. I had my little Casio out and was playing it when I walked by. Well, one of their guitar players, Jerome Dickens, happened to be outside, saw me playing, and actually took an interest this time. "What you playing?" he asked.

I said, "I told you: I play piano. I could play your keyboards. I know how to play and want you guys to give me a shot."

He said, "Alright, Shorty, we're gonna give you a shot. We got this piano down here, but if you can't play, we taking your Casio!" That was Harlem for you.

The stage was set. I had a lot riding on this audition because that keyboard was everything to me, but I was confident, and said, "Alright, try me out." They had me come downstairs into the basement. I didn't know what to expect when I walked in, but I was like a kid in a candy store! There were organs and synthesizers of all kinds, and I'd gotten lucky that day because their keyboard player had pretty much quit coming to rehearsals, so they were actually looking for a replacement.

Well, as soon as I sat down behind one of those keyboards, they turned it on for me, and the first thing I asked them was, "What key do you all play in?" That must have impressed them because one of the band members looked surprised and asked me, "You know your keys? How did you learn your keys?" I told them I'd learned from a book (as opposed to the truth, which was that I'd learned them on my own). They told me to play in E-flat, and my mind suddenly went, "Oh my God, what's E-flat?" I knew all the major keys, but this was a more specialized key to play in, and I only played by ear.

Thinking on my feet—I had to! I was afraid they were going to take my Casio!—I quickly figured out that E-flat was the black key before E. I played some major chords and minor chords, and then launched into Earth, Wind & Fire's "Reasons" with the rest of them.

But even after that, they insisted, "We still don't believe you," though I think they were actually impressed. They challenged me again and said, "Here's another song we want you to play," and launched into "Slide" by Slave, and after they heard me get through that one, the mood shifted among the group from skepticism to *Oh my God! Holy shit!*

It was funny to me how ecstatic they got, which was precisely the reaction I was hoping for, and better yet, the next thing they did was invite me to join the group, right there. They voted the old keyboard player out and me in *unanimously*, which as you can imagine gave me a huge confidence boost, being only twelve years old, where these guys were in their late teens. They might as well have been grown-ups to me at my age. The next thing I asked them was, "If the old keyboard player's out, what are you going to do with his key- board?" They said, "We're keeping the keyboard. It's ours." Instead of taking mine that day, they wound up taking his, and that's still funny to me to this day.

My mother used to always joke that "Total Climax kidnapped my child!" I remember her walking around 129th Street in tears one day because she couldn't find me. Somebody saw her and told her, "He's down with the band in the basement. He's teaching them music down there!" When she stormed down the stairs to see what was what, we all stopped playing, and she said, "I should put you in jail—you all kidnapped my child down here!"

Jerome Dickens, the guitarist, replied, "Mrs. Riley, don't punish him. It's our fault. He knows everything about music, and we wanted to see how he played." She must have been a little impressed, too, because instead of hauling me home and reddening my backside, amazingly, she let me join the band.

◆ ◆ ◆ ◆ ◆

When I joined Total Climax and started getting to know my new bandmates, immediately there were two members who stood out to me. One was Jerome, the rhythm guitar player. The other was

Michael Kim, who was the lead guitarist and, for all intents and purposes, the leader of the band. He was a big-time hustler and owned most of the instruments in the band. He even went out and bought more keyboards for me to play on after he asked me if I could play two keyboards at the same time, and I said, "Yes, if you give me time to practice." He told me I could come down there and practice anytime I wanted.

At that point, being in Total Climax became a full-time gig for me, and I finally felt I was on my way into the record business. I became so dedicated that I started ignoring my school friends because I was practicing every day after school and on weekends, just 100 percent committed to my dream. I sensed they were maybe a little jealous about that, too, because when I came around my block one day with the band, my classmates started throwing eggs at us. I was even called a "fag" and a "punk" by some of my brother's friends because of how we dressed, since it was flashier than what they could afford. I mean, I was walking around the projects at twelve in my first fur jacket. That definitely brought out some envy among the local neighborhood kids who I grew up with.

Still, I was willing to take the flack because I knew this was a once-in-a-lifetime opportunity for a kid my age. Once the members of Total Climax took me under their wing, I was learning something new every day about how being in a real band worked. It was an education for me, and important to my development as an eventual band leader in my own right. Back then, though, I was just happy to be given the chance to elevate my game, and most importantly, to be on stage playing full-band gigs. I remember being thirteen and performing at my Uncle Willie's club, Jock's Place, when everyone in the crowd was an adult. Uncle Willie had said to the band, "I'll let you guys play in the bar with *the kid*, but somebody gotta have some kind of guardianship over him or he can't come into the bar. And if the police come, we gotta take him downstairs to the basement."

Jerome would act as my guardian at those gigs—that's how I got to play in nightclubs so young. They dressed me in a little white suit with a little red shirt just like them.

It was exciting playing in front of adult audiences, and I was proud when people compared me to a little Prince or Michael Jackson, both of whom were heroes of mine. That kind of ego boost is incredible for any kid at that age, and I fed off the confidence. I was grateful not only to the guys in Total Climax for giving me a shot like that, but also to Uncle Willie, who, though he wasn't my blood uncle, played a hugely important role mentoring my career in those early days. He bought me my first Fender Rhodes and drum machines from Sam Ash, the iconic New York music store. Uncle Willie essentially adopted me, acting both as a father figure and as my guardian angel. I felt like God had sent him down to protect me when I was out in the street. Being a high-ranking hustler and shot caller in Harlem, he had the juice to put the word out and keep me from getting jumped by those jealous kids in my neighborhood. He was connected enough to get me out of trouble with the police, and later on, would protect me at my most vulnerable point in the music business. Spending as much time as I was now rehearsing with Total Climax, I was happy to have some older males in my life. I had grown up without my real father around much, though my brother's father was in the picture as a father figure of sorts, and so were a bunch of "uncles" around the neighborhood who looked out for me, not just Uncle Willie, or going back even further, my step-father, Edward, who I consider to be my real father because he was there. He bought me my first keyboard, that little Casio, and my first drum set. Throughout my childhood, everybody who saw my talent seemed to want to invest in it, helping my mother provide me with those essential instruments she couldn't have afforded on her own but knew I needed to keep expanding my musical gift.

My mother at this point was also 100 percent behind my accelerated development as a musician because she could see my talent starting to shine. She always told me I was going to be a star one day, and now saw that I was being taken seriously by professional musicians and club owners. Perhaps most importantly, because she came to many of my gigs, she knew that the audiences who were listening to me play, both on stage and even in our own housing projects, always went *wild*. It was funny, because for as many kids as might have been jealous of the music I was making, after a while, I had an equal number of fans in my neighborhood.

I lived on the first floor in the projects, and my bedroom was my studio. Locals and residents—both kids and adults—started gathering outside on the sidewalk and grass and listening as I began to write and produce music. I always thrived on an audience and would keep my window open while I was working on songs. I loved when people would see me playing and making records. They would dance and cheer me on. It proved to be good training for the career I had coming.

◆ ◆ ◆ ◆ ◆

With all the attention I was getting from female fans, it wasn't long before I first discovered sex. I was thirteen years old when an uncle of mine, who had noticed all this local fandom from the girls, said to me, "I know what I need to do with you, to make you grow up. You're a young man, so I'm going to bring one of my girls around." One day he told me to show up at the building he operated out of, and when I first walked inside, one of his workers said, "He wants to see you." I thought I was in trouble, but when I went to his office, he said, "I got you something for your birthday," and my eyes lit up. When I asked what it was, he said, "I got this girl. You're gonna meet her, she's gonna show you what to do, and you're good to go."

I remember my heart was racing like a beating drum. Looking back on it now, I was so young by today's standards, but not for Harlem in the early 1980s. If you were a player of any kind, females were inevitably attracted to you, and sex would eventually find you, even if you weren't looking for it. Sure enough, when that moment of fate arrived for me, my uncle gave me a condom, and I went in there with the girl. All I remember was her being a very beautiful Hispanic girl. I never saw her again. That was my first time, and so many musical inspirations sprang from my first time having sex. It awakened something in me as a songwriter that would mature in time as I became more experienced and I would pour that into the songs I was writing.

My reputation around the projects as a musical prodigy continued to work in my favor when it came to gaining attention from women. There was Dana, my grade-school crush, and Kathy, Tamika, Lisa, Cookie, Bebe, Michelle, and Pinky—these were all girls who I grew up dating. But my first real, official "girlfriend" was a lovely lady named Nicole. She was the first girl that I took to my house and introduced to my mother. Even though we broke up soon after that, when she moved to Baltimore, she would play an important part in my life years later in 1988 when we hooked back up and she gave birth to my eldest daughter, Deja. Being as shy as I was throughout my childhood, I welcomed the huge role music played in opening the door for me to female attention—not just for the obvious reasons that any young teenager would, but for the *inspiration* it gave me as I started writing songs.

There's always been sexuality in my music, but sensuality, too, and the more intimate time I spent with girls (and eventually grown women while still in my teens), the more I learned about how they felt, smelled, thought, laughed, cried, orgasmed—every emotional point of view that I would write from in future songs, I learned from those experiences. They taught me to think roundly as a songwriter, to be able to approach an experience from both a male and female viewpoint, and how to express lyrically what was inspired in me musically.

CHAPTER THREE

Kids at Work and the Rooftop

"I was looking at this little twelve-year-old boy playing keyboards and I remember saying to myself, 'Damn, this little dude got talent!'"

—ANDRE HARRELL, MUSIC EXECUTIVE
AND COFOUNDER OF UPTOWN RECORDS

Not many people know this, but my first major foot in the door into the music business wasn't through the studio with Total Climax, but actually as a star in a music group modeled after New Edition called Kids at Work. It was the creation of Gene Griffin, a manager, club owner, and record promoter whom I'd first met when I was fourteen and still playing in Total Climax. Even before I met him in person, I knew who Gene was—he was impossible to miss because of the flashy red Porsche he drove around Harlem.

To keep it 100 percent real, back then, when my bandmates in Climax weren't playing music, they were full-time hustlers and had our whole block sewn up, so a couple of the guys—myself included—used to wash cars right in front of that building we practiced in to earn money to buy more instruments. Then next door, the guys had a little convenience store where you could buy normal bodega stuff, but also the stuff used to mix the product. This was all run by Michael Kim, our band's leader, whose nickname back then—correctly—was The Captain. He owned pretty much that whole block, and in all of the basements, he had something going on. He was like my big brother, so I never wanted for anything. Anything I needed, from clothes to new musical equipment, he had my back.

Gene used to drive up to 127th Street to get his car washed, and while he was waiting and shooting the breeze with Michael, I would run to the store for him and get him whatever he needed. He would always tip me five or ten dollars, which was a lot of money back then, so he made an impression on me even before he'd taken an interest in me musically. Well, as he became more and more a regular face, he'd also started listening to us rehearse, along with another car wash regular named David Hyatt, who drove a dark blue Porsche, and later went on to discover R. Kelly. David remained one of my closest friends and "uncles" even though he was locked up for much of my career until his death. Loyalty is very important where I grew up, and David always watched out for me back then, and I'm proud to have remained loyal to him throughout my career.

Still, it was Gene who one day came downstairs and listened to us rehearse while he was getting his car washed. He was totally fascinated by it all, and declared, "I want to sign you all." He took a special liking to me because after getting to know all the members of the band, he saw something in me.

This was back in 1983, when I was sixteen. Gene was always a fly guy. No one knew how to dress, articulate, or be styling like him, and he was someone we all looked up to as a father figure. Hindsight being 20/20, some could argue I was signing a deal with the devil (we'll get to why those suspicions were legitimate before too long). But being green and wide-eyed, eager for a shot at the big time, I would have probably signed everything short of my soul away because I wanted so badly to be a star.

Gene first signed Total Climax with his Sounds of New York label, but that same year, he decided to start a spin-off group with me at the center of the band as the lead singer—that was Kids at Work. We started off as a cover band and did a lot of Michael Jackson and Jackson 5 songs and a lot of talent shows at schools. Soon I left Total Climax entirely to commit myself fully to Kids at Work and to sign with CBS Records.

We held the signing ceremony in the living room of my mother's apartment as she and my family looked on. It remains one of the proudest moments of my life. Because I was still a minor, my mother had to cosign the contract. I felt like we were signing it together anyway, because she had always been my biggest fan, and I knew this was our shot to make a better life for the family. Having her in my corner has always meant the world to me, and as I became more successful throughout my career, seeing her beam with pride at my accomplishments was always an extra motivator for me, especially back then, when I was just starting out.

Even with everything I'd already seen and experienced playing with Total Climax and Kids at Work, I was still naive about the way the record industry actually worked. I could see that although my mother was consenting to my signing a deal with Gene, she didn't have a great deal of trust in him. She would look at him suspiciously out of the corner of her eye, then look at me and smile because she could see how excited I was. She knew this had been my dream since the age of five, and she wasn't about to get in the way of that dream coming true. Years later, I would come to understand why she was wary of him. Back in the moment, though, this was my first real shot at the brass ring, and it was smiles all around the room. Our first and only studio album was eponymously titled *Kids at Work* and was released in 1984. It featured singles like "Sugar Baby," "Singing Hey Yeah," and "She's My Baby." It was super exciting recording my first studio album, and even though our singles were only really local hits, it gave me my first taste of visualizing stardom for myself. And now that I'd made one album, I could definitely make more.

CHAPTER FOUR

The SHACK Crew

*"The crack epidemic had particularly devastating
effects within the African American communities
of the inner cities by causing the increase of
addictions, deaths, and drug-related crimes."*
—ENCYCLOPEDIA BRITANNICA

I wish I could say that being in the studio kept me off the streets
and away from the hustling world, but by then, I had already
started hanging out at the *real* Harlem World, which was a club
owned by a guy nicknamed Fat Jack. My friends and I used to go
there a lot to see the DJ battles, and back then, I could be found in
the street—in between band practice, shows, and recording sessions—
selling drugs as part of a crew called the SHACK Crew. The SHACK
Crew were like my street brothers, and they became family when I
was around thirteen years old, which was when my father and mother
separated. Back then, I was doing everything: I was playing with the

23

band Total Climax in the basement but wasn't making any money at it, so I took time out to go down to 119th Street and Lenox Avenue to make some money.

In my mind, everything I did, either with music or on the streets, was to become popular, as strange as that sounds. So I thought selling drugs would make me popular, and it did—a little. Everybody locally knew who the SHACK Crew was, so everybody from the SHACK Crew got girls, and that's when girls from around my block started liking me—it wasn't *just* the music. Meanwhile, the money I was making started going toward helping to keep the family bills paid, which only made me grind that much harder.

We called it "grinding" back then, because the definition of the word "hustler" was someone who worked hard, getting it in. Even though the spot where I sold drugs was five blocks from my grandmother's house and five blocks from my mom's house, I never let them know where the money came from. I kept telling my mom, "I'm selling papers on Sunday," and she would say, "Papers don't bring you this much money!" So I kept bullshitting her: "I'm making money from shows, too." But she was smart and didn't always buy that line.

This was a variation on a classic conversation that a million other inner-city kids had with their mothers when they were sneaking off after school to hustle on the corner. In my mom's case, she wasn't even thinking about drugs, because her reply was, "Well, you better not be stealing from nobody," and I said, "Nope, I'm not stealing." She chose to believe that line until she caught me.

One day, my sister ratted on me about some chemicals I had in the house refrigerator, because I used to make PCP, and my mom used to always come in the house asking, "What is that minty smell?" The minty smell was the actual angel dust juice, which is a mint juice mixed with PCP. Back then, people smoked dust, and there was another apartment kitchen where me and my crew would go to cook it, bag it, and then go out and sell it on the block.

Some days before school I'd get up extra early, and my mom would think I was headed out the door for early study hall. Instead, I'd hit the street and sell at least about twenty bags, because the best time frame was 5:00 to 7:00 in the morning when people were first hitting the block to head to school or work. So I'd get down there early and get twenty bags off quick, then run to catch the 2 or 3 train downtown, then transfer over to the A or the D train to make it in time for first period at 8 a.m. at Martin Luther King High School in Lincoln Square.

I would do homework on the train or at the building where we sold drugs, wherever I could. I knew what I was doing was wrong, but the money came too fast to stop and think about that too much. And while all that was going on, in my musical mind, I was always writing music. I had new music playing in my mind all the time. I would hear beats with fully written music on top of them, and looking back on those days now, it's crazy how much was going on in my head at once. Truthfully, that is part of what made me eventually stop dealing drugs, because I said to myself, "You need to be home making beats, not out here on the streets."

When I was hustling, I had someone over me that I worked for, and we all knew how firm the higher-up-the-food-chain hustlers were with their two main rules: Don't get high on your own supply and don't be a snitch. All of that code and culture sank into my head, and I wrote about it in my music. See, when you have street knowledge, it will filter down to someone who is influenced by your music—that's a lesson I learned very young. People would rather listen to what you learned from the streets than what you learned in school. They want to hear the street knowledge, and I carried that with me into the music business; the edge in my music came from who I was on the block.

With the SHACK Crew, even though we were a hard crew, we were a bunch of dancers too. As the classic adage goes, "We hustled hard and played harder." We were all great at performing street dances, doing the Electric Boogie and break-dancing. We came up on break-dancing and moves like "The Wop" and we would work those moves in around our hustling. Our biggest day to get paid was Friday night, and this actually led to a little art-imitating-life moment when I got the idea for one of my earliest New Jack hits, "Just Got Paid" by Johnny Kemp.

Friday was the night when we had the most customers, and I came up with that song in my head while I was out there hustling. That's what I called a "corner record," which meant the hustlers would bump it while they were out there putting in work. "Go See the Doctor" by Kool Moe Dee, which I wrote and produced, was a corner record as well. I got the idea for that one because when we were out there on the corner, there were girls who would come around because they wanted to be a part of the SHACK Crew. Some of them would sometimes mess around with everybody in the crew. Well, in that case, some unlucky guy from the crew would inevitably wind up catching an STI, and he was the guy who had to go see the doctor. I always used protection back then, even with my girlfriend, because I was conscious of the risks, but "Go See the Doctor" was an all-too-familiar street term.

After months of running with the SHACK Crew, the day inevitably arrived when I finally got busted by the NYPD on a drug sweep. They rounded us all up and took us in to the Twenty-Third Precinct. I tried to act tough like I wasn't scared, but the truth was I was terrified. I got arrested at 4:00 in the afternoon and they kept me there all night, till 8:30 the next morning. While I was there, they fingerprinted me and did everything they would do for a felon, no doubt in part to scare me. For some reason, I felt like, *They didn't get me. God got me.* I took it as a sign anyway, and it eventually led me to leave the street game and to do something with my life.

I remember sitting in that chair in the precinct for hours with the handcuffs on my wrists, till this one policeman came over and began asking me questions. The first thing he said to me caught me off guard: "I can't believe you are here." It was like he knew me, though he didn't. The next thing he said was, "What do you want to be when you grow up? Because I see something in you." So I told him, "I want to be a star." I'm not sure if he thought I was being a smart-ass, because he said, "What do you mean, you want to be a star?"

I laid it all out for him: "I want to be a singer, a star, a songwriter. I wanna make music."

He didn't laugh at me. Instead he took it all in, then hit me with the cold-water question: "How you gonna make music when you're out here on these streets? You're gonna wind up in jail or dead."

I decided to be totally honest with him: "What I'm doing out here on these streets is different from what they do. Somebody has to go out and help my mom. This is how we survive." From the expression on his face, I could tell it was clearly a story he'd heard before.

Still, he paused for a moment, and then poured another cold bucket of reality on my head: "I hope that you get it together, because if you come back up here a second time, you're not getting released. If somebody doesn't come and pick you up tonight, you're going to get a taste of the real world, because you're going to Central Booking with all these kids who are doing worse things than you're doing right now. We have young kids that are killers, robbers, and what are you gonna do when you're in there with them? You're gonna have to fight them and defend yourself. Are you looking to get into the ring with them?" Then he tried to appeal to my conscience: "You just got caught with drugs, but you didn't rob anybody. You robbed society by selling drugs. It's like robbing a child or the person who's using this stuff."

I knew right there that this was my wake-up call, because I'd never thought about it like that before. On top of that, my mother had to come down to the station and pick me up, and you best believe I promised I'd never do it again. I could tell she was deeply disappointed in me, and beyond the usual ass-whooping and accompanying lecture about the danger I was putting myself in along with those I was selling drugs to, she reminded me I could just as quickly be flushing my music career down the drain. What if I'd been tried, convicted, and sent to prison, or shot and killed, my dream dead before it ever had a chance to dance?

After that, I went out on the corner at 119th and Lenox one more time out of necessity, because I'd been arrested with a lot of bags on me and now I owed a debt to my dealer. On the street, hustlers don't care about excuses: If you owe money, you better come up with it, one way or another.

I took one last shot on the corner, went out with one hundred bags, and made up my debt, plus a little extra money for myself, and after that I left it alone. I really had no choice because that last time I was out selling, my mom happened to go up to my grandmother's house for a visit and for some reason, she decided to walk back along Lenox Avenue. Why she chose that route that day is still anyone's guess—maybe she was just suspicious of my promise that I'd stopped—but she caught me on the corner herself and believe me, that was my last bust.

CHAPTER FIVE

"Don't Nobody Touch Shorty!"

"I'd listen, and at first I said, 'This is not a teenager making this kind of music—that's bullshit. So, who's really doing it?'"

—BARRY MICHAEL COOPER,
SCREENWRITER OF *NEW JACK CITY*

My ground-zero headquarters back then was a studio Uncle Willie had built for me in the upstairs office of his famed Harlem club, the Rooftop. Willie decided he wanted to make the downstairs into something more like a club, so they converted it into a roller-skating rink—basically a big open wooden floor, and you'd skate around in the section where they'd put cones down, and later in the night they'd pick up the cones and convert it into a dance floor. But the upstairs was still an after-hours spot.

Around this time, for reasons we won't go into here, the building passed in ownership from Willie to another player named Gusto. Gusto, who would become another of my "uncles," was one of the leading hustlers out in the street. (If you've ever seen the movie *New Jack City*, the club in the movie, the Spotlight, is like the Rooftop when Gusto took it over.)

The upstairs after-hours spot became Gusto's office, and along with Greg Marius, Gusto and I founded Rooftop Records, my first record label. At the time, Greg was a young rapper who had recently started a basketball tournament called the Entertainers Basketball Classic, a tournament famous in the Harlem projects because the best basketball prospects from all over the city would come and play on opposing teams sponsored by different hustlers, including guys like Willie and Gusto. Working out of Gusto's building meant I was backed and surrounded by these types of heavy hitters in the Harlem hustler trade. Everybody knew that these hustlers were investing a lot back into my musical development, and it felt like the whole neighborhood had our back.

That local legend only grew when, at the end of 1986, we established our production company Rooftop Records in the upstairs office where I started producing artists, while downstairs Gusto had the club going at the same time. With the help of Greg and Norby Walters, a major booking agent, Gusto started bringing in artists to perform on Saturday nights, after skating, so you'd have dancing and then the show. It was *the* place to be on the weekends, the club where everybody who was anybody in the game came to "see or be seen," as they say.

All the drug dealers wanted to be where the pretty girls were, and the girls would come because they knew the drug dealers were there. You had a lot of people who didn't even skate at all, and when the others would stop skating at around 12:30 or 1:00 a.m., the dance floor would open up and there was always a DJ booth and a stage where people would perform. Salt-N-Pepa had their very first show there in 1985, back when they were called Super Nature, and I would play keyboards for a couple of the acts, so everybody at the Rooftop knew me as that "little music kid."

My studio upstairs at the Rooftop was where we would go every night after we'd finished performing. We'd take our instruments up to the studio and continue working on music for my own group or whoever I was producing for—there were always new artists rolling through, trying to get on tracks I was making there. That was when I first started experimenting with making hip-hop beats.

It's also when I first came to understand, hard, what hip-hop meant as a lifestyle, which drew me in that much deeper. I was right in the middle of it, like this little street reporter taking notes on everything and translating some of that sonically, where the tough edges of the beats were concerned, and some of it lyrically and vocally, in the way I found myself at fifteen, sixteen years old beginning to direct other singers from these local groups on how to properly lay their vocals down on tape while we were recording.

It was an incredible way to teach myself the art of producing records, and we used to laugh whenever Gusto would bring in a new piece of equipment to the studio, often purchased at my request but sometimes something he'd heard about, like a new sampler that another competing studio was using, maybe the E-mu SP-1200 or the Roland TR-808 or other drum machines you'd begin soon enough to hear in my earliest rap hits in 1985 and 1986. The joke was that no one else knew how to use any of them, so whenever we'd get a new piece of gear in, this excited group of tough guys would be like kids huddled around me, an *actual* kid, watching as I played around with it, testing out new sounds on tape as I was teaching myself how to use the machines.

It was like a dreamland for me whenever I was up in that studio or on the stage, absorbing everything from the hustler lifestyle I was seeing and hearing around me and then pouring it into the sound I was crafting that would eventually be known as New Jack Swing. I began developing the roots of that sound long before it hit the airwaves, and my proving ground whenever we'd finish a new tape was to test it out on the block. I'd make a bunch of copies on a dual cassette stereo system that Gusto had bought me and then take the tapes we'd dubbed and, in old-school hip-hop style, sell them the very next day out of the trunk of our cars and on the block. It was amazing: Just hours later, you could walk up and down the streets in Harlem and hear those *same tapes* being blasted out of boom boxes. It was an incredible laboratory for me to experiment with—I would create new sounds, get feedback from the hustlers on the street, and then go back into the studio and continue to refine what came to be my signature sound and style as a songwriter and producer.

Even after I took myself out of direct danger from selling on the street and plugged full-time into making music, I was still at risk. Growing up in Harlem at the height of the crack epidemic, you were surrounded by trouble. It came for me one night when I was still in my teens and I literally saw my life flash before my eyes, just as things were about to really begin to take off for me.

I wasn't the target; Gusto was—but I wound up in the cross-hairs. This was 1986 and the Rooftop was now the hottest club in Harlem. We'd just started Rooftop Records the same year. Still a teenager, I was head of production at a company in partnership with Gusto, Greg, and my friend Lavaba Mallison, who would go on to become a big manager in the music business. Gene Griffin was now in jail, convicted on tax evasion charges, of all things. (That should have been a sign of things to come.) I had left Kids at Work by then, back in 1984.

Uncle Gusto had made similar changes to mine, leaving the street life and investing his proceeds fully in the Rooftop's various enterprises. But there is always a problem when someone in his position makes an exit like that, especially if they go out as successfully as he did, with rumors floating around that he had divided several million dollars among his top street partners and another $250,000 among some mid-level lieutenants. By Gusto's math, he had fairly compensated everyone and he moved on with his life. The problem turned out to be twofold: First, word had gotten out that Gusto had big dollars, and second, anyone who was interested figured the most likely place he'd keep that money was in the safe in his office, upstairs from the club.

Jealousy and the gangster mentality made for a dangerous cocktail, and it all exploded one night while we were upstairs working: me, Timmy Gatling (from Kids at Work), Lavaba, and Greg, while Gusto was back in his office taking care of one kind of business or another. We all had our guards down, music blasting. Timmy was about to head downstairs when a gang of masked, gun-toting jackers came bursting through the door.

Timmy angrily yelled at them, "What's going on?" not realizing, I think, that they were strapped, and in response, they pistol-whipped him to let him know they meant business. In fact, they cracked him in his ear so hard that it ruptured, to the point that it looked like it was falling off. Blood was everywhere. Seeing that, along with the guns, shot the fear of God through me. All I could think to do at that moment was to pray silently, because I thought we were all going to die that night.

They were pointing those barrels at all of us, yelling, "Get down on the floor!" They forced us to lie down side by side in an office across from Gusto's. A couple of the gunmen kept the hardware trained on us, while the others were in Gusto's office screaming at him to give up the cash. Gusto kept pleading with them, "You don't have to do this," and they kept yelling at him, "Where's the money at? Where's the safe at?"

They next marched him into the office where we were all lying on the floor, and threatened to shoot us one by one if he didn't give it up. It was clear they were intent on killing him, because where I grew up, you don't rob someone like Gusto for that sort of money and leave him to talk about it, or to seek revenge. The same street rules would then apply to witnesses, meaning us.

Gusto kept insisting, "You don't have to do this—ain't no money in here!" The rest of us were all praying quietly. It felt like time stopped at that moment: I could hear my heart racing, but no music was playing in my head. I was afraid I'd never make music again, never see my mother and brother, Markell, again, never live to see any of my musical dreams come true. These fears were flashing one by one through my mind as I prayed harder and harder, along with the rest of the guys. One of the gunmen yelled down to us, "Shut up!" But God must have heard us praying, too, because what happened next was nothing short of a miracle.

We were all lying on the ground. Timmy still had blood gushing out of his ear and running down his face, and I had turned my head to the side. As a result, the gunmen could actually see my face. I remember thinking maybe they'd have some sympathy for me if they saw how afraid I was. They all had bandanas or ski masks covering their faces, so all you could see was their eyes. The scene felt right out of a movie, looking back on it now.

At this point in my life, while I wasn't famous yet, I was pretty well-known around my hood from being in Total Climax and Kids at Work. That ended up saving my life. Suddenly one of the masked gangsters cut in and blurted out, "Yo, that's Shorty!"

As soon as I heard that, an instant rush of relief overcame me. *I might have a chance to survive this!* Another gunman began arguing with the guy who recognized me: "What are you talking about?"

The first guy yelled back to him in an even more forceful voice: "Don't do *nothing* to Shorty. That's that little music motherfucker! *Don't do nothing to Shorty.*"

It turned out that at least one of the robbers was a fan of mine. We worked out later that he must have come to the Rooftop previously and seen me perform there with Kids at Work or F.A.M.E., another group I had going. Talk about relieved: These cats had AK-47s and nine-millimeters pointed at our heads, and they were getting angry enough to pull the triggers because Gusto wasn't telling them where the club's safe was. Gusto finally gave it up and told them, "Alright, I'll take y'all where the money is."

Instead of shooting us, the gang of robbers told us to stand up, and they then locked everyone in the studio bathroom, except for poor Gusto.

The gunmen warned us that if anyone came out, they'd shoot

us all. After a short time, thankfully, we heard them exiting through the club's loud steel storefront gates, but we still waited another ten minutes or so before looking to see if it was okay to come out. I was relieved but of course very shook up, especially because sparing my life hadn't come for free. I was fat with between $5,000 and $10,000 in cash I'd just scored from producing a record for the group World to World, and the gunmen had jacked that. Worse still, when they were rummaging through my pockets, they swiped the keys to a black Volkswagen Jetta I'd just leased. Luckily, they didn't kill Gusto when he finally agreed to take them to where he kept his money, but he got jacked too.

The experience definitely left us all a little scarred, literally in Timmy's case, and not only his ear: If you meet him today, you can see the split in his lip where he also got hit in the mouth. In hindsight, we were all extremely fortunate to walk out of that situation with our lives because the same crew of guys wound up on an episode of *America's Most Wanted* about a year later for pulling a similar heist. A big drug dealer named Kevin Chiles had just come home from jail and immediately became a target. The crew had gone over to Kevin's mother's house. She had nothing to do with his business and was home having her hair done. They ended up killing the mother, the lady doing her hair, and three other people in the house.

After the robbery, I moved all my equipment out of the club and set up shop back at my apartment, because I no longer felt safe recording at the Rooftop. My mother's living room was now my musical ground zero. I still shake my head when I think about her allowing me to take over like that, but it was yet another indication of her belief in my growing talents. Plus, after hearing about my near-death experience, she was happy to have me somewhere safe.

◆ ◆ ◆ ◆ ◆

My studio setup back then centered around a very classy-looking wooden jukebox that had been in our living room since I was a small child. In fact, I believe we were the first family in my projects— probably the only family—that owned a real jukebox. It had a lid so you could close it, and I would set my keyboard, drum machine, and tape machine on top of it while I worked. I'd gotten a hold of a Teac tape machine from Total Climax's soundman Newbie—who we called Mr. Nebulas—who'd first loaned it to me until I'd gotten the money together to buy it outright from him. He had introduced me to the art of recording and taught me how to engineer. We also moved all the other state-of-the-art studio equipment that Gusto had invested in over to my mother's apartment, the new home of Rooftop Records. I didn't just feel safer at home; it actually proved to be a smooth business move too.

See, though being based out of the Rooftop had given me a certain aura of heightened respect because of how official that setup looked, the fact that I wasn't out in the streets anymore had temporarily created a bit of a bubble around me. I was removed from it all, but that was what originally had inspired me so deeply. Being based at home, I was right back in the St. Nicholas projects just as a new generation of East Coast superstars were about to begin blowing up and blazing new musical trails.

Growing up in Harlem in the 1970s and early 1980s, I was on the ground floor of hip-hop's birth as a genre, which started, in a lot of people's minds, with "Rapper's Delight" by The Sugar Hill Gang, which came out in 1979. I was already making records by then, still in my early teens, and had seen and sensed that rap was going to do something to the world because of the reaction it was getting on the streets.

This was before hip-hop had really reached radio, and it was right around the time when I'd started DJ-ing with my two buddies Freddy and Freddie in the park and at house parties in the projects. I was twelve years old when I first started listening to rap, and the Freds were only a few years older than me. Even after I got into Total Climax and Kids at Work and moved away from the DJ-ing gigs, I was already hooked on making beats of my own. Before long, word that I was making beats had gotten around to the other local hip-hop artists who were starting to come up.

By the time I'd moved my studio back into my mother's apartment in 1987, I was producing tracks for everybody around the neighborhood, and now I was doing it out of our living room. I'm talking about making songs for some of the major new rap acts of the day, from F.A.M.E. to Schoolly D, Busy Bee, and on and on.

Then one day Doug E. Fresh came to my house and everything changed forever.

I'd first met Doug after I was kicked out of Martin Luther King High School for getting into a fight with a guy in a class of mine. A bunch of us were joking around with one another, throwing erasers at the chalkboard, and this one kid ratted on me to the teacher. That was a no-no where I came from, and when I caught up with the kid after school—I had all my friends with me, who were the worst of the worst by reputation—I had to fight him. I threw the first punch and hit the kid dead-center in the middle of his nose and broke it. Then everybody in my crew got in on the action and stomped him out. Well, that only made things worse for both of us because all his front teeth got broken out of his mouth, and when word got back to the powers that be, I was expelled because the school administrators wanted me to name everyone involved, but I wouldn't do what this kid had just done and tell on my friends, no matter the cost.

I still remember sitting with my mother up in the principal's office and the principal saying to me, "Who was fighting with you? Because you didn't do all this by yourself, Mr. Riley."

My mother warned me, "Boy, if you don't tell on somebody, you're gonna get kicked out of this school!"

In front of both of them, I said, "Mom, I'm not a snitch. I'm not going to tell on anybody. It ain't just going to be about getting kicked out of school. If I tell on any of my friends, I may get hurt—they know where I live—so I'm not going to do that."

In my neighborhood, there was nothing lower than a rat, and it always caught up with you. Snitching just wasn't in me anyway, so I took the fall for everyone, and getting expelled was the price I paid.

After that, I got sent to a tougher school, Park East High School, which was for kids who'd gotten kicked out of their regular high schools. I was worried it would be too wild for me, but it just so happened that Doug E. Fresh went to that school. I didn't know who he was at first, and he didn't know who I was, but everything happens for a reason, and within a couple of weeks, later in 1985, we wound up making "The Show" together, which played a huge role in launching both our careers. But even before we'd recorded together, when we were still classmates, I started hanging out with Doug E. and the Get Fresh Crew, and Slick Rick.

I initially came up with the beat you hear on "The Show" after Doug had played me a demo he'd made in his music teacher's classroom. It had the general concept for "The Show," but I felt they had too many commercials crammed in together, so along with the beat, I added the *Inspector Gadget* theme to the song as well. Luckily, back then, all the copyright infringement laws weren't in place yet, so you were a lot freer to use samples in songs, and once I added the *Inspector Gadget* sample to what they already had with Doug E.'s beatboxing, I pulled out my Oberheim DX-7 drum machine, and, to top it all off, I added those low shakers you hear in that instrumental, which was actually the birth of the New Jack Swing sound.

CHAPTER SIX

A Mother's Memories

BY MILDRED RILEY

When I was younger, I always would say, "I'm going to Hollywood." I even did an audition and got a call to come read a radio announcement, but my husband wouldn't let me go. But I sang all my life, and when I was pregnant with each of my kids, I sang. Going to work, I sang; coming home, I sang.

When Teddy was four, my brother was staying with us and he had a guitar, and Teddy would sneak in and touch his guitar. My brother would holler at him, "I told you not to touch my guitar," so one day after it happened again, he got mad at Teddy and told him, "You want that guitar, then go sit down and play it right now." Teddy sat down and played a song by Jimmy Reed. My husband was in the other room and he'd heard all this, too, and he came in and said, "If he's that good, he's got a gift. I can tell he's got a gift," and he went to the pawn shop and got a trumpet, came home, gave it to Teddy and said, "If God gave you a gift and you're musically inclined, blow this trumpet," and he blew it, and that trumpet was bigger than him!

At first, we started buying my sons toys, but they'd always lose or break the toys, so we started buying them instruments. Teddy got a drum, and my daughter got a keyboard, and my other son got a horn, and Teddy could play around on all of them. If you remember those gramophone record players with the turntables up on the top, well, he was about nine, and I came into the living room from my bedroom and he was sitting there singing "Chain of Fools" by Aretha Franklin, and I said "Baby, what'cha doing?" and he said, "I'm trying to sing like the record!"

In my house, we played music all the time because my husband had a jukebox, and on the weekends, I used to cook dinner and we'd host a poker game from Friday to Sunday, sometimes even into Monday morning. I'd cook and sell dinner to the players—I'd make collard greens, red rice, potato salad, all that, and we'd start the poker game and have the jukebox on and when people weren't playing poker, they were dancing. When these games were going on, I didn't allow Teddy or his siblings to be in the room. But I knew he and his little brother were always peeking in from around the corner, wanting to come out and perform for those folks. Teddy never did get along with anybody that was his age; he was always drawn to adults.

He first started out in church. I had told him when he was younger, "If you don't go to church, you don't go outside to play." Every Sunday morning when he was younger, around eight or nine years old, I would say, "Teddy, why don't you play the piano for the church?" and even though he was shy, he said, "Okay, Mom."

Then one day he said to me, "Mama, how come that man gets more time up there and I can play better than him?"

I said, "Baby, you know, he's an old man and he's just working because he's on a fixed income and trying to make ends meet. But God's going to bless you. You just take what he gives you and he's going to bless you much later on."

With that, he played for my choir in church, and every Sunday, he went to Universal Temple and played over there. We prayed for him and encouraged him to keep on going.

Teddy could have been a drummer. He played the drums in grade school, and he used to go to the auditorium and fool around on the drums. His music teacher caught him one day, and when he asked him what he was doing sitting up there, Teddy told him, "I can play the drums," and he said, "No, you cannot play these drums," and then Teddy said, "Why don't you try me out?" and the music teacher finally gave in and said, "If you're going to bother me that much, here, why don't you take these sticks and beat that drum," and he beat that drum! So they had a concert in school one day. I'd come straight from work to listen to him play because he'd told me, "Mama, they're giving a play, and I'm beating the drum. Please come and see me." I was five or ten minutes late coming through the door, but when he saw me, he got that smile on his face, and boy, he wailed on those drums.

When Teddy joined Total Climax, their guitarist, Jerome Dickens, told me, "Mrs. Riley, we're giving a concert at the club." I said, "Yeah, but Teddy's too young to go," and he said, "If you signed me as guardian, I can take him with me, and you can come too." So I went and had a good time. Eventually I named Jerome guardian, but I told him, "If you want Teddy practicing here all the time, you've got to tutor him, and he's got to do his homework and be ready for school in the morning." I believed enough in Teddy to let him take that chance. When he played onstage with them, even back then, he looked natural up there. They dressed him in a little white suit with a little red shirt, just like them.

But none of us could keep our eye on him all the time, and it was hard competing with the draw of the streets. Like so many boys of his age, Teddy was impressionable, and would often run the streets, and someone said to me one day, "Mildred, you better go get Teddy off 119th Street."

So I told my son, "Teddy, I don't want you on 119th Street no more," and he said, "I'm not doing anything, Mama." One night, I was going to sing gospel at church because I was on the program, and I told my friend on the way, "Drive to 119th Street because Teddy ain't home, and I told him not to be down there," and sure enough, who do I see on 119th but Teddy!

Well, I rolled up on him and said, "When I get home, you better be there," and who wasn't there when I got back? Teddy didn't get home till 2:00 or 3:00 that morning, and oh, when he got home, I had my little belt, and he and I had a good time. Then he grabbed that belt out of my hand and said, "You ain't hitting me no more!" and God must have put power in me because all I know is I had him on the floor and said, "And if you don't tell me you're going to stay off 119th Street . . ."

My son Markell remembers that I'd do all that to Teddy and yet he'd go back and do the same thing all over again. But all of us have seen the belt! Some of us have seen it more than others, and Teddy had his fair share of the belt because he wouldn't listen. My husband and I had separated by then, but he still watched them, and my friends out there watched them, so when they said, "Mama, how you know all this?" I'd say, "Hey, I know everything," because I had sources who would come and tell me. And I thanked them for it; I didn't ever argue with them and say, "Oh no, my child don't do this" and "My child don't do that." I didn't want my kids handling no drugs, peddling no drugs or nothing, so therefore, I was always keeping an eye and ear out.

One afternoon, I got a call from the police station, and the officer said, "You need to come down and get your son." I prayed all the way down there; I was calling Jesus. I got down to the police station and thought he was in big trouble. Instead, all the police officers were standing around in a big circle, and Teddy was in the center talking to them about his music.

♦ ♦ ♦ ♦ ♦

I remember that Teddy ran in the house one day and said, "Mama, I made twenty-five dollars!"

I said, "You made twenty-five dollars?!" and then he said even more excitedly, "Listen to the music, listen to the music!"

When I heard "The Show," I remember being impressed, and asked, "You did that?"

He said, "Yeah, Mama, I did that, and he gave me twenty-five dollars."

Then I responded, "He ain't giving you twenty-five. You go back there and tell him to put your name on that record, and that you want royalties."

So Teddy went back, and Doug E. was very nice about it. It was clear to all of us that Teddy's music was going to be his way out of poverty. There was no question in my mind he was going to be a star. I just did my best while I was raising him and his siblings to keep them on the right track along the way to getting there.

CHAPTER SEVEN

How Ya Like Me Now?

" 'The Show' would not be what it is without
Teddy Riley. That's factual, and I say that because
sometimes we get caught up in thinking we did
it all ourselves, but we never do it all ourselves.
In this particular case, I have no problem giving
credit to someone who has made a contribution to
something that has changed the course of hip-hop."

—DOUG E. FRESH, RAPPER,
PRODUCER, AND BEATBOXER

I was seventeen when "The Show" was released in 1985. It was an important step forward, for me, for Doug and Slick Rick, and for hip-hop at large, as it would turn out. But the moment I first felt New Jack Swing taking form as a full sound was when I did "Go See the Doctor," by Kool Moe Dee. Lavaba Mallison, who had survived the near-fatal robbery with me at the Rooftop, had first brought Kool Moe Dee to my studio. We all lived in Harlem, but I'd never crossed paths with Moe before. He was already a local star, as a member of The Treacherous Three, and signed to Sugar Hill Records.

When Lavaba introduced Kool Moe Dee and me, it felt like one of those special moments for any producer where you hear a voice that sounds natural over your beats. That day I happened to be working in a studio in New Jersey, which was in the basement of a friend's house. He played for Con Funk Shun, and had an 808 drum machine there. We made "Go See the Doctor" on that 808 the first day Moe and I ever worked together. Though I'm usually the beat-maker in the room, I'm happy to open my ears to whatever rhythmic suggestions my collaborators have when we're working on a song. Moe started beatboxing a beat idea out to me, and immediately I programmed it on the 808.

I asked them to come back a few hours later, and when they did, I already had much of the musical track together for him to rap over. I played the song's bass line on a little Yamaha DX-100 keyboard and had quantized the drum pattern and put it in the Swing mode, which Moe *loved* once he heard it. I explained that what we wanted was a street record that people could still dance to. That combination was a bedrock of my production formula right there, and it's what I think made my music connect so instantly with those who first heard it locally, before I'd even launched on radio. One funny moment in that song comes when you hear me going, "Skeeza, ungh, come on, Skeeza!" We knew we had something truly special by the end of that first session working together.

As Kool Moe Dee recalled, "For me personally, 'Go See the Doctor' was the hardest record for me to write because it was the easiest record to write. I had to put no real thought into it: It literally was a story about me and a friend of mine sleeping with the same girl and me going to the doctor because he said that he got burnt. I wasn't, but in the waiting room, I wrote the idea for 'Go See the Doctor.' Teddy made all the difference with my getting on radio for the first time."

When that was released in 1986, it was the biggest street record for every neighborhood, every ghetto, everywhere—everybody was singing "Go See the Doctor." Between that and Doug E. Fresh coming out with "The Show" just months earlier, my beats were ringing ears all over Harlem. That was when I first heard my music really influencing the streets and knew that this music had so much of an edge on it, because the streets—especially my streets—were loving it. At the Rooftop, "Go See the Doctor" was an anthem.

People don't realize it, but it's not just like I produced these guys, got my check, and that was it. I had a vision with Rooftop Records that tracks like "Go See the Doctor" captured perfectly. In fact, Moe and I got along so well that he left Sugar Hill Records and we first released the single at the Rooftop, after which it immediately became an underground hit. It got so hot that soon enough Jive Records picked it up, and Kool Moe Dee signed with them. I was happy for him and knew it would be not only a springboard for his career, but also a shot for me to elevate my own to that next level of visibility, a national level, because Jive was an important label with a connection to Clive Davis and Arista Records.

Soon, "Go See the Doctor" started getting played on the radio locally and nationally, and I was proud that it got from the streets to the radio. The first day I ever heard it on legendary local R&B radio station WBLS, I was stunned, but quickly recovered and yelled out, "Mom, my record's on the radio!"

Back then, we used to have local block parties where the whole neighborhood would come out to listen to the DJs, who would all bring their turntables and PA systems to throw a live concert. All the local rappers on the rise would come out and rock the mic, and the year "Go See the Doctor" and "The Show" dropped, both Moe and Doug E. showed up to play for the crowd. It was amazing to be on the stage playing along on my signature keyboard. I would rock the *Inspector Gadget* theme on Doug's song and the crowd would go *nuts*.

Soon, both records caught on nationally, and I went from hearing my songs on the radio to watching them be performed on MTV. Moe and Doug were natural stars on screen, and my music was the soundtrack to their success. Moe wound up with a platinum album, his self-titled first LP, which earned me an invitation to London to produce his second album, *How Ya Like Me Now*. That trip would change my life. It would introduce me to major music executives without the interference of my local partners, who had their hands in my pockets.

On that point, I'd like to clear the air here on a common misconception among music historians: Gene Griffin is popularly credited with discovering me, and that's true for me as a musician and performer. But it was a record executive from Jive Records and its parent company, Zomba, by the name of Clive Calder who I credit with recognizing my talents as a producer. Clive is the guy who first discovered that I was the one actually producing and making the beats for the first Kool Moe Dee album.

Thanks to Clive, I was whisked off to London to work on Moe's second record. I was personally excited, because this was my first time ever leaving New York City, let alone the country. Professionally, I was excited because I was being flown to England and paid to do what I'd been doing in my projects living room only a few months earlier. Moe had a budget of $10,000 from Jive Records to make *How Ya Like Me Now?*, the only catch being that they insisted we record at their label-owned facility, Battery Studios, in London.

Moe flew us all over to London in July 1987 for what would be my first-ever time in an airplane. We recorded nine songs in total, over approximately three weeks, and we had all the inspiration we could ask for given the state-of-the-art music environment. I felt like a kid in a candy store. The studio had rented an Akai MPC-60 drum machine and though I didn't know anything about it when I first got there, once I got my hands on it, I taught myself how to use the gadget in less than an hour. The engineers and everyone else at the studio were amazed at how quickly I picked it up.

Back then, I had all my sounds and samples on floppy discs. This might sound funny to any of you Millennials or Gen Z kids reading this, because you've probably never heard of them, but floppy discs were these flimsy, paper-covered magnetic discs that were used to store digital info in those days. I used them with my Korg DDD-1 drum machine, and that's how we started work on *How Ya Like Me Now?* before I learned how to use the MPC-60. Once I'd mastered it, I took all my sounds from the DDD-1 and imported them into the MPC. My preference was getting the sounds on there, all the hits, because I didn't produce any of my sounds on the keyboards—they just didn't have a keyboard that could sample that long. I was making those sounds on the drums, processing the bass drum, and then next thing you know, I had all these kick samples.

That was the magic of the sampler: It allowed you to dig into the crates of old records and take pieces of the musical past, whether it was an obscure sample from a 1940s jazz record or one-shot hit samples from James Brown, and blend them all into the new, modern sound of New Jack Swing (even though it didn't have a name yet). Those were the samples that I put in the drum machine, and that's how the title track "How Ya Like Me Now?" came about, and then I added the horn sounds from the Yamaha DX-7. It was done with only those two pieces of equipment: the MPC and DX-7.

A key moment for my own career's rise came one day at Battery Studios working on the album when Clive walked into the control room. He saw me alone at the console but didn't really have any idea who I was yet. Sure, we'd met on the plane over to London, but there were a lot of guys in the entourage. But that day, all of the other guys were out to lunch, while I had stayed to work on the beat to "How Ya Like Me Now?" I still remember this guy just standing behind a window looking in at me, watching me work. He had this funny, quizzical look on his face.

For my part, I was thinking, *Who's this guy looking at me?* I had no idea he was the CEO of the label and publishing company. He kept looking and looking, and then actually started dancing, moving and kind of shucking his body, so finally I stopped, because at that point, I was thinking, *Either this guy's going to say something to me, come inside, or I guess stand out there and keep looking at me.*

After a while, he finally walked in.

"Lavaba?" he asked.

I replied, "No, my name is not Lavaba."

Then he looked genuinely confused, and asked, "Who are you? Where is everybody?"

I said, "I'm Teddy Riley."

Still confused, he asked, "Um, so you make the beats?"

And I replied, "Yeah, I make the beats. I'm making the beat for this record right now, and I'll have it done by the time they're all back from lunch."

Next, he started asking me a bunch of questions: "What beats have you made?" and "What else have you been working on?" Then abruptly he said, "I'll be right back," then apparently went up to

57

his office and made a call to the label's office in New York, telling everyone in the office, "I wanna talk to you about that kid making the beats for the Kool Moe Dee album—I had no idea who he was." This is what he told me afterward, once we got to know each other. He told me he felt like he'd found an entirely new sound, an entirely new *genre*, in the music he heard me playing.

Once he returned from his call upstairs, he put me through what felt like either a job interview or an interrogation. He kept asking me questions and then finally said the words that changed my life: "We're interested in signing you. What other records have you produced?"

I told him, "Well, 'How Ya Like Me Now?', 'Do You Know What Time It Is?,' 'Wild Wild West,' and 'I Go to Work,' all by Kool Moe Dee. I also did 'The Show' by Doug E. Fresh and the Get Fresh Crew."

As I was talking, his eyes got wider and wider, and by the end of the day, he'd signed me through Zomba to my first music publishing deal.

I was so happy, getting my first real break with the publishing deal, because here's the truth: With my Kids at Work record deal with Gene, I hadn't seen any money come across my palms. Everything went through Gene. The difference with my publishing deal with Zomba—which I signed independently from Gene—was that I soon saw my first real check in the record business. The amount was substantial, and I wanted to understand exactly what the check was for. Clive happily explained to me that it was an advance against the royalties I'd see from music publishing revenues that would spring from the songwriting side of what I did in my capacity as a producer. More importantly, and even though it was a 50/50 split with Zomba, it was money that Gene couldn't touch; it was mine and mine alone. At that time, I didn't have *any* money, so it was something tangible. In hindsight, I know I gave up a lot, but I got in the door. It was like a price of admission, just a *big* price.

CHAPTER EIGHT

Guy and Uptown Records

"When I signed Guy to Uptown, I was excited to be working with both Teddy and with Aaron Hall. Teddy Riley gave R&B a new groove, and Aaron Hall gave it a heart because of the way he sang those songs—'Goodbye Love,' 'Let's Chill'—he gave a real romantic and soulful vocal to put on top of that go-go-meets-R&B-meets-hip-hop sound that Teddy was creating. But see, Teddy didn't just make music; Teddy made a whole musical lifestyle: He took Harlem to Paris and Japan. He's the soundtrack to Ghetto Fabulous. He's absolutely 'The King of New Jack Swing.' There has been no one else, since Teddy, to make a sound with a lifestyle that kept the same swagger as the hustlers, even though we took that and flipped it to something legal. That was an amazing, amazing time, and it would not have happened without Teddy Riley."

—ANDRE HARRELL, MUSIC EXECUTIVE AND
COFOUNDER OF UPTOWN RECORDS

Though I'd been in groups like Total Climax and Kids at Work, I had grown comfortable behind the boards, writing and producing songs for other artists who I was molding into stars. And my first priority was to stay on the charts. So the idea of starting a new group was *never* on my radar, until one day when I was actually working with Heavy D in the studio and Timmy Gatling was hanging around, helping out with some of the vocal tracking. Timmy, a year older than me, had grown to be like a big brother to me, and a good friend, so I was pleasantly surprised during that session when he first came to me with the idea of forming Guy. (Kids at Work had long since broken up, around when Gene Griffin had been sent to prison for a couple of years on tax evasion charges.)

By then I was getting calls from everybody in the business asking me to work with them, and felt I'd found my true calling: to become the next Quincy Jones. It occurred to me that to be known and seen, maybe joining another group wasn't a bad idea, but I didn't want to force it.

The next time Timmy brought the idea up with me, I was working on a Keith Sweat album in New Jersey, and he turned out to make what proved to be a fateful trip out to the studio with my future bandmate Aaron Hall. Timmy and Aaron knew each other

from working in the women's shoe department at Abraham &
Straus, a Brooklyn department store, and they had written some
music together.

When they got to the studio, I immediately took to Aaron's
voice. He didn't say much, but he played the piano and sang. By
then, I'd become an expert at instantly recognizing a platinum voice,
and I immediately said to myself, "I want to work with this guy." I
didn't know that Timmy had brought him with the idea of us all
three being in a group, but that night, the idea began to take shape
as Timmy started talking again about starting a band.

He's not recognized enough for it, but Guy never would have
existed without Timmy, and from the beginning, he quarterbacked
the vision for the group. Even if I didn't want to be in it, he told
me, "You'll produce it." But the project almost derailed when Aaron
piped up and said, "I don't want to do a group." Maybe he had his
own plans in mind to be a solo star, or already had some sort of singing duo going with his brother Damion, who I hadn't met yet. But
then he surprised Timmy and me both by giving his condition for
joining: "If I'm gonna do a group, I want him in it." He meant me.

I was flattered that Aaron thought that much of me musically.
He didn't really know who I was yet as a producer, but he'd heard me
play piano that night, so artistically, there was a mutual respect. And
when Aaron said that, I replied, "Cool, I have some connections. We
should check out Gene and see what he's doing, and I know we can
also go see Andre Harrell and he'll probably give us a deal because

my next projects are both for Uptown, Heavy D and the Boyz, and Al B. Sure!"

At that point, Gene had just gotten out of prison after serving his tax evasion sentence. We went up to meet with him at a hotel off Central Park, and he was eager to get back in the business. His eyes went green when he met the members of Guy, and when we took him back up to my mother's apartment, after he heard what we were working on, he said, "This is incredible! I want to sign you. Let's make this thing happen. I think we can do a deal." So once I made that hookup between Gene and an already very excited Andre Harrell, the deal for Guy with Uptown was a no-brainer for everyone involved.

And we did do a deal, but the funny thing by then was that it actually happened because I introduced Gene to Andre Harrell at Uptown Records, who had already been producing records for us while Gene was away. The fact that I was the one making things happen didn't matter, though. Gene was a gangster, and, back then, he had us signed to a dictatorial management and production deal that we couldn't escape from, no matter how popular we got.

I just kept focusing on the music, feeling like with every hit I made, I was getting my family further and further away from poverty. In 1990, I was finally able to move my mother, brother Markell, and the rest of our family out of the St. Nicholas projects and into some much nicer condominiums—in fact, in a crazy coincidence, my condo was the very same one that The Notorious B.I.G. and

Faith Evans had lived in previously. Still, I couldn't yet seem to shake Gene's mafia-style tactics, the way he kept his tentacles wrapped around me—and in all my pockets. That's how it truly felt, like if I had a Rolex on my wrist, Gene had a matching one on his, and *I paid for both of them!* Gene was like my twin in that respect: If I wanted a new Benz, he got one too. It was crazy the shit he got away with!

Once we'd signed the deal with Uptown, Gene started trying to sidle up to me every chance he got, because word had gotten around while he'd been upstate about how the records I produced had started to blow up on radio, and he was determined to have his taste. The proof of that? Gene actually had his own production company, G.R. Productions, which stood for Griffin-Riley Productions, in which he and I were supposed to be partners. I say "supposed to be" because according to Gene this was a verbal agreement, but it was never put down in writing anywhere. That didn't matter with the "street way" that Gene did business, where if you gave him your word and a handshake, it was as solid as a legally binding contract as far as he was concerned.

That didn't stop him from laying claim to me as soon as he got out of prison, even though I'd done *all* of the work by myself to get my name out there during those years he was incarcerated. Nevertheless, if you take a look at any Guy record, Gene Griffin is listed as a cowriter or coproducer, even though he wasn't involved in either process at all. He even went as far as to "legally" add himself as a fourth member of the band, contractually. He had barnstormed into Andre Harrell's apartment one morning at 7 a.m., getting physical with Andre and demanding rights to my publishing. Andre, frightened by Gene's muscled-up ex-con intimidations, wound up signing my publishing over to Gene. No matter how much higher up the proverbial ladder I seemed to move in the business, I just could *not* seem to get this guy's claws out of me.

Gene really was the Suge Knight of the 1980s, given the way he strong-armed his way into the business. After Andre had made that first concession and signed my publishing back over to him, next Gene wanted to get us *out of our deal with Uptown*! Andre went to meet with him at the offices of MCA Records, and Gene actually slapped Andre at one point during the confrontation. Gene wanted total control, and he even showed up at the IMPACT Convention as a second round of putting fear into Andre and his crew. Andre responded by bringing along a former enforcer for Nicky Barnes, the notorious 1970s Harlem drug kingpin. The enforcer now worked for Priority Records, and he stepped to Gene and cooled things down.

That might have helped Andre keep us signed to Uptown, but it didn't help me get Gene's one hand out of my pocket and the other from around my throat. Everything was moving so fast with Guy that Gene was able to keep us in a kind of work bubble while he committed highway robbery. No money went straight into my pocket because Gene had it set up so that every cent went through him first. I never saw accounting statements or bank records so that I could see where my checks were being deposited or what was coming in every month.

By then, I had hits all over the charts, and even though I'd been able to move my family to a condo in the suburbs, I wasn't living near as large as Gene. Finally, one of Gene's workers, who I guess was too big a fan of mine to keep watching this go on, basically sat me down and broke everything down for me. I was heartbroken once I understood the vast extent to which this guy was in control of my career. It turned out that Gene was taking my money as it came in and investing it into all kinds of other things, some of which were illegal, including money laundering. He was taking our advances from Uptown and putting them in his own pocket instead of into the album. For example, we didn't even record the first Guy album in a professional studio. Believe it or not, even though we theoretically had the money to book a studio like Chung King or Media Sound, the record was made back in my apartment and then finished up at Sound Works Studios in the basement of a building right next to Studio 54. We set up our studio in the living room, with the bathroom acting as a vocal booth.

The first song we came up with for the project was "I Like." Timmy had come in with the first part of the verse, and then Aaron started elaborating on it, and I was playing the keys. Usually, Aaron would come in with a melody or a piano part, and I would expand on that, taking the song to the next level. Once again, every song on that album was written solely by me, Timmy, and Aaron, but Gene added himself as a cowriter, even though he didn't contribute a single musical note to that album.

Music was the only thing that kept me sane back then, between the demands being put on me within the studio and now, with Guy, on stage. The pressures of producing hits in the studio and the stresses of then having to go out and sell them as stars are *radically* different. I had signed up for the limelight, but it was hard at times not to get totally lost in it. I never used drugs or even drank. This issue was more balancing the pressures of all the music coming out of my head with the demanding production schedule I was juggling between working with Guy and all the other artists I was writing and producing for. And then there was also Gene's ever-looming shadow in the background.

Once we'd wrapped the principal recording on the first Guy album, we took it downtown to Sound Works. Upstairs in that same building was another studio called AXIS, where we were also comped a lot of free studio time by the owner, Uncle Willie Brewington. The funniest thing was, once we took what we'd been recording at my mother's apartment studio and tried to re-cut it in the real studio, we couldn't get anything to sound the same sonically or instrumentally, so we then had to transfer all the original tracks from my AKAI 12-track, because there was simply no way to duplicate that sound.

With the studio's 24-track, we could stack more background vocals and make the sound bigger, and that's what we did. But we also preserved the initial raw authenticity of our music. So I guess the world owes Gene Griffin a thank you, in a roundabout way, for stealing our studio budget and keeping us from making the album in a fancy state-of-the-art studio; if we'd done that in the first place, maybe we would have lost some of that street edge within our sound.

Sadly, just as we were finishing our first self-titled album, Timmy quit the group, which was a huge letdown because his passion and talent were among the main reasons I'd formed Guy with him in the first place. The way it went down, I was in the studio tracking a vocal with Aaron while Timmy and Gene had been out in the lobby arguing over who was running the show. Timmy had *balls*, trying to be the voice in the band fighting for us, but Gene told him, "Listen, I run the show! Everything's going to go my way, or you're going to have to hit the highway," and Timmy did just that. I was shocked and heartbroken.

At first, I didn't know exactly why Timmy had left the group. He simply came back into the studio, gave me a high-five and a hug, and said, "I'm outta here."

I was stunned, so I naturally asked Gene what had happened, and he just said, "Everything's good, man." That made no sense.

"What do you mean?" I asked.

He said, "Timmy doesn't want to follow my rules, so he's out of the group."

It's funny thinking now about "Gene's rules" because, again, it wasn't Gene but *Timmy* who had first brought Aaron to me, and who had been instrumental in our starting Guy. After Timmy left, I continued making music, but I was sad every day doing it without him. Gene being a street chess player quickly saw this as an opportunity to assert further control over the group when he and Aaron decided to replace Timmy with Aaron's brother, Damion, who Gene then signed to some sort of similarly draconian management agreement.

When I let Damion Hall become a part of the group, it was pretty much because Aaron had gotten me to agree to it, but it never occurred to me that this would upset the group democracy, and that in time, the Halls' majority rule would overpower me. Damion was let into the group solely because of Aaron, and we didn't even know exactly what he was going to come do musically, just that we needed someone to fill Timmy's spot (if that was even possible). For me, there could never be a comparison between Damion's contributions and what Timmy Gatling had brought to the group. To keep it 100 percent real, Guy was never the same after he left.

CHAPTER NINE

Keith Sweat
and Bobby Brown

"Teddy came up with 'I Want Her' right in his living room, in the projects. He would say, 'Sing it like this,' and hum certain things out. That's how we would work with each other: I would hum him something, and he'd come back like, 'Something just ain't right,' and so he'd come up with the chords on the keyboard. Then certain tracks he would just create himself, and I would say, 'Yo, I hear this on that track,' and we would make magic together. The chemistry was so crazy that it was ridiculous because we were just coming up with hit records, every day. He trusted me and I trusted him, so we never questioned each other in terms of what we heard or felt musically, because we both were good at what we did."

—KEITH SWEAT, SINGER AND SONGWRITER

t always makes me proud when I hear songs I produced forty years ago bumping out of car stereos or pumping in clubs today. One example is "I Want Her," which I wrote and produced for Keith Sweat in 1987. It would become my first Top 5 hit on the Billboard Hot 100 Singles Chart and help give New Jack Swing its first national exposure. More recently, it's racked up over 22 million plays on Spotify. It was history-making when it dropped and still stands the test of time today.

I'd first met Keith while I was still in Kids at Work and we performed in a competition against his group, Jamilah. It was a small world, and that's how Keith and I started making music together. He lived around the block from me and was known around the neighborhood as that kid always making music—just like I was. But Keith was older than me and had signed with Elektra Records through a singles deal he'd struck with a smaller label, and one day, he came to my projects and said, "I wanna work with you, and get some of that music from you!"

My first reaction was, "Man, I don't make R&B music. I make rap music." This was when I was with Kool Moe Dee, which was easy money for me. It was like the street game: I started out getting $25 for a beat, but soon I was making $1,000 a song—and this was all back before I was twenty-one yet. But, in an effort to expand my listening audience and reach new ears, I changed my mind about working with Keith, and we wound up recording his entire first album, *Make It Last Forever*, at my studio in my mother's apartment.

The way I put the combination together, if you listen to "I Want Her," for instance, it's not on the same line as the keyboard: My production philosophy was that you didn't want everything to be the same. It's almost like not matching clothes when you're putting together a wardrobe: You don't want to be wearing all black straight down, hell no. Instead, I think of what I'm going to *contrast* with the black. It's the same thing with music: I have the drums going one way, and I'll have the keys going another way that I want them to pair with the rhythm. Or I might have pads (chords or tones) going while the rhythm is going, and then take that bass and go somewhere else completely with it compositionally in the song. So if you notice, all my music is kind of unorthodox. It's like kung fu, karate, and jujitsu—mix them together, and put in anything else you want.

When I made "I Wanna" with Keith, and then "Just Got Paid" with Johnny Kemp (who was performing at the same competition where I met Keith), I was using that same drum machine I used with Moe, the Korg DDD-1. Back then, we recorded vocals using a Shure mic that looked exactly like the ones they use at radio stations. I had to leave Keith bare because when you add an effect like symphonic or chorus to a voice like his, which has so much vibrato, it doesn't sound right. With Keith, I did use reverb, for something that's a small-voice plate reverb effect, which makes the sound of his voice a little wider. We knew we were on to something that no one else was doing, and that we felt in our hearts everyone would want to hear once it hit R&B radio.

Keith and I used to drive around together dreaming about everything we were going to do once we made our first million dollars. That's the sort of thing hungry artists coming up out of the hood will do, especially when your star is on the rise. Keith used to tell me every day we were in the studio that he knew this album was going to be a hit because we were turning them out every session. And it was literally only the two of us: me creating all the musical performances and him giving me platinum vocal after platinum vocal.

From the opener, "Something Just Ain't Right," through to the closer, "Don't Stop Your Love," *Make It Last Forever* was one of the first albums to lay hip-hop beats underneath R&B music and vocals. Just as importantly, much of the music was not sample-based but my own original compositions. We worked for six months on that album, recording nearly twenty songs before we winnowed it down to the best ten.

Working with Keith was a big deal for me commercially because it marked my first success writing and producing an R&B record. That experience made me realize that there were so many musical styles out there I could be working in, from hip-hop to R&B to pop. I felt like it was suddenly all out there just waiting for me, a whole new sound I could already hear starting to come out of me in the records I was writing and producing myself.

"Just Got Paid" was actually a demo from the *Make It Last Forever* sessions that we didn't wind up feeling was quite right for Keith, but it proved to be perfect for Johnny Kemp, becoming his breakout single when I was in the studio with him working on his *Secrets of Flying* LP. Ironically, Johnny had done the demo for me while the song was still intended for Keith, and his scratch vocal was so electric that we wound up keeping it as the final vocal you hear on the record, which hit number one on the U.S. Billboard Hot R&B/Hip-Hop Songs Chart, as well as the U.S. Dance Club Songs Chart. It also became another Top 10 hit for me on the Hot 100 Singles Chart. A funny footnote, thanks to Gene Griffin's strong-armed thievery in his publishing deal with me: If you look on Wikipedia or Allmusic.com or even the album itself, the credits list *Gene* as the cowriter with Johnny, even though I wrote the majority of that track with Johnny. Gene had *nothing* to do with it whatsoever.

I made peace with that years ago because my fans know who wrote all of those songs, but to think that so many stars, songwriters, and producers were robbed for years by paper gangsters like Gene and Morris Levy is just a truly sad chapter in the history of the music business. Chuck Berry talks in his Taylor Hackford–directed documentary *Hail! Hail! Rock 'n' Roll* about being victimized by the same sort of thievery, and sadly, even as late as the 1980s, this sort of larceny was still allowed to go on in plain view of the music-buying public. Anyone who worked with me knew Gene had nothing to do with helping me create any of the music I made, and if they looked at *Billboard*, though they would have seen his name in parentheses as a cowriter on my hits, they would *know* it wasn't true. Looking back, I wish someone had spoken up on my behalf—I was still a kid!—because it cost me *millions* of dollars that no one ever advocated for me. Thankfully, things have changed over the forty years since, but ripped off or not, I'm proud of the fact that Keith and I were making musical history with that album.

By 1988, my New Jack Swing sound was starting to tear across the nightclub scene and urban radio and video as well. Everyone covering music, metro, or culture was writing about how people were going crazy for New Jack Swing. Back then in New York City, whether you were turning your radio dial to 98.7 FM or WBLS 107.5, you'd hear Keith and Johnny rotating around the clock, but it was Bobby Brown's "My Prerogative," released in October 1988, just as I turned twenty-one, which really put my sound on the map. I remember the now-legendary session with Bobby as a lesson in the importance of being firm and fearless as a producer, no matter the status of the star with whom you're working. Usually, the tension within that creative back-and-forth produces something truly inspired, which helps make a song into a hit.

"My Prerogative" was actually a song I produced *way* before, and it was supposed to go on the first Guy album. I wrote "My Prerogative" with Aaron. I'd come up with the beat, which I played for him, then said, "I've got this hook," and ran that down for him, too. Then Aaron started singing the verse melody: "Everybody's always talking, all this stuff about me, why don't they just let me live?" So he was singing it just like you hear in the finished record, and once he sang that first verse, I then answered him with, "I don't need permission, make my own decisions . . ."

Aaron and I cowrote the lyrics, vocal harmonies, and vocal melodies (and later Bobby added some ad-libs of his own), but I wrote all of the instrumental and production elements of the song you hear playing underneath, including the beats. I played the signature bass line you hear in the opening on a DX-100, which was my main keyboard by then, and later the D-50 as well. Aaron and I were originally supposed to sing it for the Guy album, but Gene told us, "It's too late, bro." The record was already being mastered. So when Bobby Brown came through the projects looking for me, we had this song already finished, tailor-made for him. It was like fate.

We thought we were handing him a hit on a platinum platter. And he loved the original demo when we played it for him at my house. But once Bobby and I were in the studio tracking his vocals, something wasn't right.

Either he got a little intimidated or possibly, in the back of his mind, he thought, "People know me from ballads like 'Girl Next

Door' and 'Girlfriend,' that type of stuff, not this." He clearly wasn't comfortable at first and wasn't delivering with the attitude we needed from him. So I told him at one point, "Bobby, you *want* people to know you as something different." I was so sure in my producer's gut that I doubled down: "If you can't do it this way, then it's not gonna work."

Well, *that* didn't work. He actually said, "Alright, I'm outta here," and stormed out of the studio.

Bobby was so mad at me that he called his label, MCA, to complain. I later heard that Louil Silas Jr.—the label head—wouldn't have it. He allegedly told Bobby, "If you don't get back in the studio, we're going to shut your project down. You need to get in the studio with that New Jack Swinger. Do you understand? Anything he touches turns to gold, so you need to get your butt back in the studio!"

A couple of days later, Bobby came back in the studio and sang it the way I told him, but I could still tell he wasn't totally feeling it. Things came to a head again when it was time to record the bridge, where he launches into the famous rap: "What is this, a blizzard, where I can't have money in my pocket and people not talk about me? . . . I don't know what's going on, I got this person over here talking about me, this person . . ."

If you listen to the final song, you'll hear that he ends the bridge rap sequence with "Right, Ted?" Well, initially, he didn't end the vocal rap with my name, and we didn't get that on the first rundown because it wasn't part of the original lyrics. At that point, he was still mad at me, and I could hear it in his singing—he wasn't fully in it. I knew we were *this close* to having a number one hit on tape, so I put my psychologist hat on, brought him into the control room to hear what he'd been singing, and said, "You need to listen to this."

When he came in and listened, everybody looked at him and said, "Teddy was right: This is the new you." Something switched on in his head right there because he started believing in himself. He started believing what everybody was telling him, and that sparked a moment of inspiration that helped make the song, because the next thing Bobby said was, "Alright, I got something else."

First, Bobby went outside and smoked a joint, and when he came back in, he was much more creatively energized, and said, "I wanna sing it down; I just want to do some things and throw some stuff in there, ad-libs and whatnot."

So he did the whole song straight down in one take, and that's where I got that, "Yo Teddy, kick it like this, oh no no, I can do what I wanna do, me and you . . ." and then the signature outro line: "I made this money, you didn't, right, Ted?! *We outta here!*"

All of that came out in his ad-libbing, and it brought even more life to the song: "It's my prerogative, can't you see baby doll" and, near the end of the song, "Why you wanna talk about me? Tell me, tell me"—all of that was Bobby riffing. (As an interesting footnote, that's also one place where I can say Michael Jackson followed Bobby. On "Remember the Time," near the end of the song when Michael ad-libs "Remember the times, do you remember, girl," he only did that because of Bobby ad-libbing, "Why you wanna talk about me?" Michael said, straight out, "I want my ending to be like that!")

As Bobby recalled later, "I had wanted to work with Teddy for a long time, since he was in his first group, so I went to see him in New York. I loved the comradery, and that's how we started coming up with the lyrics. That's what gave us the inspiration to come up with 'My Prerogative.' Then we went back to Teddy's mom's apartment in Harlem and that's actually where we recorded the demo. We did the vocals out of the bathroom—Teddy, Aaron Hall, and me. It was just a lot of fun. Teddy allows the artist to not only be themselves, but also to find different ways to use their voice. For example, I wasn't used to singing bass, to singing as low as I do on the line 'They say I'm crazy . . .' because I have such a high-range voice. So, for me to be able to use my baritone was an eye-opener for me. It was something I hadn't used before then, but it just worked. Teddy knows how to bring that out of you. I wanted 'My Prerogative' to come out first, but I think we did it the right way. The label put out 'Don't Be Cruel' and it didn't hit as hard, but then we put 'Prerogative' out and it just tore the world up! Then we re-released 'Don't Be Cruel' and it only took those two songs to start the wave of what we were trying to do."

That was the first time my bandmate Aaron Hall and I had chart success as songwriters. The Bobby Brown single went to number one on the Billboard Hot 100 Singles and Hot Black Singles charts. That radio sensation was a great profile boost for us as members of Guy, too.

♦ ♦ ♦ ♦ ♦

So here I was, producing hits for Bobby Brown and Johnny Kemp—like "Just Got Paid," where I was the *only* writer, producer, and performer, aside from Johnny and Aaron—and Gene was still getting paid behind me, somehow. It was a classic game in this business that unfortunately managers and "record executives" like Gene have been taking advantage of young and naive artists for years: It happened to Bruce Springsteen with Mike Apell, TLC with Pebbles, Jackie Lymon and Tommy James with Morris Levy, and God only knows how many others. And it happened to me, Teddy Riley. It's sadly not that small of a club, but we looked at it like this was the price of admission, similar to me having to give up 50 percent of my publishing to Jive/Zomba, but thankfully, my publishing deal had already been signed and once the label found out what was going on, they actually took Gene to court over it.

Now, you might ask: What motivation could I have possibly had to keep making music when I knew Gene Griffin was going to wind up with a sizable yet illegitimate slice of everything I made? My mentality was to take refuge in my music and pray that, eventually, I'd get so hot that I'd be able to leave Gene in the dust. For the time being, it didn't quite work out that way, but I was determined not to let him sink my ship. I won't lie, though, and say it wasn't hard at times to keep focused with an uninvited cocaptain on board, his hand constantly on my wheel. For instance, as soon as he saw that I had labels like Andre Harrell's at Uptown coming at me from every direction wanting me to produce tracks, Gene also signed on as my manager.

As a consequence, the pattern of him taking co-credits that had begun with Johnny Kemp and Bobby Brown continued with Guy, his name winding up on everything, even though he did next to nothing for us. Back then, we didn't know anything about conflicts of interest or double-dipping, while Gene was an expert. He signed his name as the fourth writer on our songs, which he hadn't had a thing to do with writing or producing, and even added himself to the Guy publishing catalog.

The next logical question: Why didn't we buck? Well, Gene was a very intimidating guy with a lot of street credibility and the ability to strike fear into almost anyone, especially people our ages, so we just went along with his extortion for a while.

◆ ◆ ◆ ◆ ◆

My next big success on radio would come via my collaboration with Heavy D & the Boyz. I first started working with Heavy when we went into the studio to make the *Big Tyme* album once he'd signed with Uptown. What got me excited as a producer and what made me take songs I had originally intended for other artists and give them to Heavy was how he pulled each number off. I don't care if you don't like it at the beginning of the record, by the end he'll make you believe—that was Heavy. His music made—and still makes— you believe *I am a star, and I am going straight to the sky and nobody's stopping me now.*

Heavy used to come and spend nights with me working in the studio, which was then located in a house I'd moved to in Riverdale, New York. We'd wake up and keep developing songs and come up with something that would shock the world. Heavy was a technician—not just a rapper—so he knew how to pull it off, whether he sang it or rapped it. Sometimes he would say to me, "Alright, there is a special style I want to do to this. I know I haven't tried it before but I'mma do it," and he just did and he made it work.

So there was nothing that Heavy couldn't do. Heavy to me was like the Michael Jackson of rap. He was one of my best friends in the business, and when he passed away in November 2011, my heart broke like the rest of hip-hop's did. I was proud that he and I were spotlighted so often together as collaborators in celebrations of his legacy, as our work together remains one of my personal and professional highlights to date.

We were prolific, too, but don't take my word for it. The *New York Times* said as much when they noted in Heavy's obituary: "Thanks in part to production from the New Jack Swing auteur Teddy Riley that matched hard-snapping drums with sensual melodies, Heavy D & the Boyz became key figures in the softening of hip-hop's sharp edges. The group released five albums between 1987 and 1994, three of which went platinum."

Heavy D was one of the most talented artists in hip-hop and that I ever worked with. He was innovating with me every time we stepped inside the studio, and I'm proud that you can still hear the reverberations of his influence in music today. He was a one-of-a-kind talent and is missed by millions.

CHAPTER TEN

The Show Must Go On

"I still remember when Teddy and I were in the studio together working on 'I Get the Job Done.' I sat there listening to the music he was making and started writing. I think maybe a couple of nights before, I had watched this Redd Foxx video where he was talking about licking women's breasts, and he said, 'Show me a husband who won't, I'll show you a n$$$a who will.' Then he started talking about how thin his lips were, saying he could hardly taste barbecue and then stuck his tongue out and said, 'But they get the job done.' Sometimes someone can say something and it will just trigger a whole entire song, and that's what made me decide to write the song, and we made magic that night."

—BIG DADDY KANE, RAPPER AND PRODUCER

We had a tour to mount and a record to promote, and Damion Hall would soon prove his value to the band with the talent he had for dancing. We used to call him "Crazy Legs" out there on stage. Gene gave him that name, actually, because Damion was always dancing. When it came to going on the road, we only had maybe four, five, or six rehearsals before we all felt like we had it. Then we shot a bunch of videos, and everyone felt like we'd made it through the worst of it, so on with the show.

The problem came with the fact that it was hard to organize a tour. Eventually we would wind up opening for New Edition. But starting out, we opened for anyone we could get a slot with who was a known recording act. Our first show, in fact, was opening for Johnny Kemp in Newark, New Jersey. He actually brought us up on stage and introduced us. The crowd didn't know who we were—they hadn't heard the record yet—and were booing us until we started "Groove Me." Then they went nuts.

Thankfully, the public similarly received our debut LP, which came out in the summer of 1988, pushing four of our singles—"Groove Me," "Teddy's Jam," "I Like," and "Spend the Night"—to numbers four, five, two, and fifteen, respectively, on the US R&B Singles chart. We reached number one on that chart the next year when we cut a track for Spike Lee's movie *Do the Right Thing* titled "My Fantasy." That one rubbed my fellow band members the wrong way because the label billed the single as "Teddy Riley featuring Guy."

MTV would later honor us for playing a key role in the "birth of the New Jack Swing movement," saying, "Their influence is still resounding today." It's funny looking back at it now, given how we worked our way up to being that big of an influence so quickly. At the height of the first tour, it got to the point that we couldn't even get in the theater for our own show—that's how crazy it soon was for us with everybody recognizing us and wanting a photo or autograph. We were it, and the first time I heard "Spend the Night" on the car radio, I was so shocked that I promptly rear-ended the person in front of me. My favorite shows from that tour began with the very first concert we headlined; it was pandemonium, it was so crowded.

That show was at the Palladium on 14th Street in Manhattan. People from across the city attended that show: Brooklyn, Queens, the Bronx, Staten Island, and, of course, my hometown of Harlem. The Palladium had to open up an exit they hadn't used in years to sneak us in, along with a police escort. The cops were talking back and forth on the radio, and one of them said to another, "I don't know who these guys are, but they remind me of The Beatles." And when he said that, oh my goodness, you could see everybody in the band's chests puff up. Everyone in that position loves to point to The Beatles as a reference, though I preferred to cite The Jackson 5 when they first became stars at Motown.

I thought *Vibe* did a nice job summing up the commercial significance of our first album in a 1988 cover story: "That year, Guy's self-titled debut album on Uptown/MCA was released, R&B was losing it . . . Guy's sound, created by Riley, and later dubbed 'New Jack Swing,' literally tore down those barriers, not by adding a perfunctory 6-bars by some rapper in the middle of an R&B song, but by placing Aaron Hall's traditional gospel voice over beats that had bounce, beats that would have been just as appropriate for Erick Sermon or Rakim. Guy's first single, 'Groove Me,' and others like 'Don't Clap . . . Just Dance' and 'Teddy's Jam' were as big at after-work soirees as they were in Jeeps on 125th Street in Harlem. And when Guy did straight R&B, they were just as forceful . . . 'Goodbye Love' and 'Piece of My Love' were more than love anthems, they were every future R&B singer's blueprint for vocal delivery. *Guy* went platinum in a matter of weeks."

The Hall brothers were still very green back then, new to success, and neither had ever been in the studio before working with me. I'd never take credit for either one of their vocal talents, but one key thing I helped mold both the brothers to do in the studio that became signature was to harmonize with each other, because Aaron had rhythm, but it was hard for him to sync with a track, so that was my expertise: showing him how to stay in the groove and know the funk. I don't take anything from him because he's a great piano player and a great singer, but making records is a different ballgame. So when it came to shaping him as an artist, yes, I did that for Aaron, and he started finding himself as a recording artist and R&B singer through working with me. The problem was that it all went to his head. But by then, everyone in that camp had grown big heads, with Gene's, not surprisingly, being the biggest.

Still, heading into the end of the 1980s, we had a lot to be thankful for. Personally, the moment that brought that home to me most profoundly how far I'd come was when we played the first of four sold-out shows at the Apollo. I remember pulling up to the gig in my white Mercedez-Benz 500 convertible with the top down. As I was pulling up to park, in the middle of the street I saw the police officer who had scared me straight after catching me hustling a couple of years earlier with the SHACK Crew. That had been a big deal because he'd told me he saw something special in me and had cut me a break. His parting words to me were, "You are going to be somebody."

To me it felt like fate that this same police officer randomly happened to be working foot patrol that night on 125th Street, helping to direct traffic. I stopped. He looked at me and I looked at him, and then I put the car in park in the middle of traffic, hopped out, and raced over to go hug that cop.

He told me, "I knew you were gonna be somebody, and I told you. Man, I'm proud!"

I said to him, "I wanted to thank you. I found out your name and thanked you in the album." To me, it was a miracle, because I could have been somewhere else that night, either on the corner or in jail or worse if it wasn't in part for that officer.

I also had my mama to thank. I called her one day and said, "Mama, I want to thank you."

She asked, "For what baby?" and I replied, "So many of the things you'd tell me I best not do or else you'll get me—thank you. Because if you didn't tell me all that and kind of scare me on the way, I would have been dead."

Amazingly, amid all the drama and work with Guy, I was still busy behind the boards where, along with Heavy D, I found time to produce two of the biggest hip-hop hits of 1989, one coming via my final collaboration with Kool Moe Dee, on the *Knowledge Is King* album, and the other via working with Big Daddy Kane on his "I Get the Job Done" single, both of which helped cement my place as one of the most influential East Coast hip-hop producers of the 1980s. Working in the studio with Kane was fun, too, because he was at the top of his game and I was at the top of mine, and as soon as we got in the studio together, we knew we had a hit on our hands.

Benny Medina, Jennifer Lopez's future super-manager, had first put Kane and me together, thinking it would be a good idea for us to get in a studio and see if we could come up with the missing single for Kane's new album. He told me at the outset that while he'd dug what I'd done with Kool Moe Dee and Heavy, he didn't want a pop or club sound to rap over. Instead, he expressly told me he wanted what I'd done for Guy. I took that as a great compliment, that our sound was already known enough to be the influence for the sound of established stars. I played him a sample from "Catch a Groove," the classic 1970s track by Juice, as inspiration, and he loved it. He took off to go shoot a scene for some movie, and building off the Juice sample, I had the instrumental track for "I Get the Job Done" done by the time he returned later that night to lay down his vocals.

When I hooked up again with Kool Moe Dee in 1989, it was like a family reunion. I knew exactly what to give Moe musically because I'd produced the bulk of his studio albums up to that point, so it was a pretty intuitive process for us by then. I was excited to see his career exploding like mine was, especially because he'd bet on me back before any of the success with Keith Sweat, Bobby Brown, or Guy. Moe was one of the first artists to take a chance on me, to take me with him to London, which led to my publishing deal with Zomba/Jive, and so it was great to be back in the studio working with him on what would be his third album, *Knowledge Is King*. He was constantly trying with each album to evolve to the next level of his career, and we both felt this one had a different sort of confidence to it.

We'd both been grateful to not have to fly back to London, as Zomba had now opened its own recording facility in New York City, and when Moe and I got in there together, once again we pulled out a banger with "They Want Money." He was answering some groupie who had claimed she was carrying his child, and it must have resonated because it climbed all the way to number three on the Hot R&B/Hip-Hop Songs and number two on the Hot Rap Songs charts. It was a smash hit in the clubs, and we even had NFL players telling us it was their favorite workout song.

"I Go to Work," the second hit we made together on the album, reached number thirteen on the Hot R&B/Hip-Hop Songs and number five on the Hot Rap Songs charts. Moe had a vision for that one, which he described to me as "James Bond meets James Brown," and when you listen to those lead descending horn notes, we definitely captured that vibe. He used to call what we did together "The Teddy Upgrade" because he would come in with a great concept or foundational idea and together we'd build it into a platinum single. Buddy McGirt, the welterweight champ then, told Moe, "When I was training, 'Go to Work' was the record I'd throw on before I hit the heavy bag!" With that one, we had another knockout hit on our hands for sure.

The cash by then was coming in like a gold rush. The only problem was, I wasn't seeing anywhere *near* my fair share of the profits. In hindsight, I recognize that in some ways, I might not be where I am today if not for Gene, but I should have been treated much more fairly financially, because I was the moneymaker of our "partnership," G.R. Productions. Despite that, I was never treated as a true partner. All I was ever given was a company credit card. Eventually, my mother threatened to go back home to the projects if I didn't leave him, so things were getting very stressful in 1990, the last year of my working relationship with Gene.

Leaving felt to me like attempting a prison break. Once I'd decided to divest myself from my "partnership" with Gene, I started meticulously plotting my escape. I first had a meeting with a girl group we'd signed called Abstrac', and then with Aaron and Damion from Guy. I also sat down with Wreckx-n-Effect, Andre Harrell, and a couple other artists and told them all basically the same thing: "I'm going to get out of this agreement. I'm leaving Gene."

When I said that, they all said, "We are with you and will support you." I also drove directly to the bank to check on what was supposedly my account, and was told I couldn't withdraw any funds because in fact, I wasn't even a signatory on the account—this was before I'd even told Gene I was leaving the company.

After the success of Guy's first album, Gene had bought houses for me, Damion, and Aaron all together down in Duluth, Georgia. Little did I know that we were living in those homes illegally through some real estate scam, so there was no security, even though I'd moved my mother, siblings, my fiancée, and my daughter, Deja, who was still just an infant, into my house as well. Gene owned all three houses, even though he'd bought them with *my money*. I knew in my heart at that point things were about to come crashing to a head.

My mama was wary. She said, "When we get there, I want to see the paper on the house. I want to see what all you own and don't own." She hired a lawyer, and she and my uncle took the lawyer down to Duluth, and the lawyer told me, "Teddy, you don't own anything. You don't own your car. You don't even own your house!"

When I finally got up the nerve to talk directly with Gene, I was so nervous I had my mother standing physically behind me. Gene was sitting in his massive office behind his big desk with all my platinum albums lining his walls, acting like Berry Gordy Jr. When at first I couldn't find the words to tell him I wanted to end things, my mom finally burst out, "Go ahead and talk to him, boy."

When I found my tongue, it all came rushing out of me, all the anger, the emotions I'd had pent up inside me: "Gene, I want out of this whole situation. I don't want to do business, I don't want to produce, I want to do nothing anymore with you . . ."

I still remember the shocked look on his face. All he could come back with was, "What do you mean?"

I doubled down: "Like I said, we want out of everything with you. We don't want to do anything else. I signed to you when I was underage, so we don't have a legal contract, and we just want out. As far as my producing career, we don't want to have anything to do with you, and all the groups—Guy, Wreckx-n-Effect—we all want out of our contracts."

Realizing, I think, that he was backed into a bit of a corner by the threat of having his primary talent leave the building, his next move was to ask, "Man, what is it that you want?"

I was on a roll at that point, with all this frustration boiling out, and the truth just took over the conversation: "*We don't have any money!* All the money that I made, you took. Everything that I rightfully own is in your name, and I don't want my business like that. I don't want to be in business with nobody under those conditions, and now I want to have my money and my name."

As bad as Gene liked to project himself to be, at that point I knew I had one advantage over him. If he'd been a boxing promoter and I'd been his top prize-fighter but told him I didn't want to fight for him anymore, even if he'd beat me up, how would he get me back in the ring if the desire was just plain out of me? As a musician, I didn't have a kid's fire burning in my belly anymore. I'd made it. I was a star by then, and I knew heading into that negotiation he couldn't take that away from me. He could take my advances, my royalties, my concert revenues, but he couldn't take my stardom. *That*, I knew, would keep shining, even after he had burned out, but I had to get free of his shackles first.

Employing the classic music manager psychology, once he got his wits back about him, he responded not with anger but with clear awareness of what he had to lose: "Well, we can fix that, man. We can make this alright—"

But I held my ground. "It's too late," I told him. "At this point, I don't care if you keep it all—I just want my life back. It feels like my life revolves around G.R. Productions when it should really be T.R. Productions, and it feels like everything revolves around you. It can't be like that no more, because I'm tired of being put out there and having nothing to show for it." Again, I made my point plain: "I have no money. You own everything."

I could see desperation starting to strain his face: "Well, I'll give you money, man, just tell me you'll stay, and I'll give you money."

From there, he started promising this and that, and when that happened, I finally said, "Gene, it's okay, it's okay. I just want to shake hands and go." Then I saw him shed a tear, and I felt like he shed that tear sincerely, but my mother didn't trust him even for that. She knew what a master manipulator he was, and she jumped in right then and said, "Gene, I didn't sign this contract for my son to be in a situation like this. I signed it trusting you, and this is what you do for my son? He has to get permission from you to spend our money?" He didn't have much to say after that.

CHAPTER ELEVEN

The Great Escape

*"Betting that the hits will keep on coming, MCA Records
has signed Riley to an exclusive five-year contract that
gives him his own label, Future Enterprises Records,
and gives MCA a huge shot of credibility in the black
music community. He says his MCA deal gives him
both more security and control over his productions."*

—*LOS ANGELES TIMES,* NOVEMBER 1990

O nce Gene and I had our big breakup, I was racing around
New York trying to figure out how to move my family back
up to the city and find them a place to stay without winding up right
back in the projects. From the bank, I'd driven to the airport and was
trying to book a ticket to fly back to Georgia on the company credit
card—the only credit card I'd ever had up to that point—when I
learned that Gene had cancelled it. I couldn't believe it. And I only

had twenty dollars in my pocket. That's when panic began to set in, with the dawning realization that what I was doing was very real.

Standing there in line at the airport ticketing counter—it was Christmas Eve, no less—the only person I could think to call was Marsha McClurkin, from the girl group Abstrac' that Gene and I had signed. She would turn out to be the true angel on my shoulder that day, because she saved my life financially after Gene shut the lights off, so to speak.

"I need to come stay with you until I make some money," I told her over the phone, my heart racing. "Gene shut down all my bank accounts and my credit card. All I've got is the twenty dollars in my pocket."

"What do you mean?" she asked. "Hold up, wait a minute! Do you have that card that I gave you eight months ago, that platinum credit card?"

This was the ray of hope I'd been praying to receive, because she'd worked in a bank as her day job and had given me a silver American Express credit card, which I'd stuck in my wallet and never thought about again. So right there, I ripped my wallet out of my pocket, started feverishly leafing through it, and sure enough, gleaming amid the thicket of endless business cards was the lifeline that saved me that day. That card had a $100,000 limit on it, and after running it, the airline clerk handed it back to me along with a first-class ticket back to Atlanta.

I was almost brought to tears talking to Marsha that day, thanking her over and over again—and even then, I told her, "Words can't express how grateful I am."

She just sought to reassure me: "Listen, go get your family back to New York, and I'll see you when you get back."

Gene naturally didn't make it very easy for me to get my family packed up and moved back north, even after we'd hired a tractor trailer the day after Christmas to pack up everything from the house next to his on the lake. I even had my gangster "cousins" from Harlem come down to work as extra security because I was afraid Gene was going to do something treacherous to us and that house, but thankfully we drove out of there with no other problems—for the time being.

It was like a breath of fresh air pulling out of there. I moved my family into a townhouse complex in Teaneck, New Jersey. It even had an elevator, so we were definitely moving up in the world. At that point, I had run through most of the American Express card limit getting my family moved back and settled, and given that it was our only source of funding, pretty soon I started to worry again about where my next record-making paycheck would be coming from, especially now that word had gotten out that Gene and I were no longer a team. The call that was my next answered prayer arrived one day from Benny Medina, who was then the president of the Urban Division at Warner Bros. Records, asking me if I'd remix "Don't Wanna Fall in Love," a top 10 hit on the pop charts by the Canadian singer-songwriter Jane Child.

Of course, I jumped at the opportunity. This was my first job after leaving Gene, and I was ecstatic to be back in the studio, this time in downtown Manhattan at Soundtrack Studios, and the positive thing for me was my music and my productions were still being heard on the radio. That was the one thing that made me feel really good during all of the drama: that my music was being appreciated and was being received by my people in New York, and that it was becoming the soundtrack of a lot of people's high school and college lives all over the country. That's what kept me going.

One day, just as I was starting to get my life back to some sort of normal, I got a call from Gene, out of the blue, saying, "What's up, man?"

I stayed cool on the phone, offering only, "Ain't nothing," and he continued, "How you making out, man?"

I said, "I'm cool, just trying to make it here," and then he—almost tauntingly—got to the point: "Well, you got some cars you need to return."

Now, these were cars purchased for me, my mother, and my brother—these were vehicles I thought were paid for with my money through the company.

"What do you mean?" I said. "These are my cars."

He responded, "Well, I'm paying the notes on them, so you gotta return them."

I was just over it by this point, because Gene was starting to act like a pissed-off, bitter divorcé. Keeping my cool, I said to him, "Gene, how you gonna do it?"

He didn't skip a beat: "Yeah, man, we ain't partners no more, so no cars."

So I came back at him with, "Well, what about the money you owe me?" and he said, "I don't owe you nothing, man."

I knew at that point I was going to have to sue him if I had hope of recovering anything.

"Okay, Gene, we're going to return the cars," I told him, figuring at this point it was better to have no ties to him at all.

Growing up, I was a little kid who knew all these big-time street guys—Richard Porter, Fat Jack, Gusto, Greg G, Little Man, AZ, Whitey, Junior Owens, Chris Washington—who had looked out for me, the guys I called my "uncles," and thankfully they still had my back when I split with Gene. I started getting anonymous calls and hints that Gene did not like how things were going down. One of Gene's people even told me directly that he was making threats against me. With tensions rising, an unlikely sit-down between me and Gene was arranged by several of my Harlem "uncles," who were there guaranteeing my safety, while Gene had his own people to back him up.

It was the kind of night and scene you could take straight out of a mob movie, only this was for real. The meeting was held at one of the most treacherous places in the city, a joint in uptown Harlem that gangsters from everywhere—Italian, Colombian, Black—frequented called the Flash Inn. I was petrified walking in, but my

Uncle Willie was the one who had put the meeting together, and his best friend controlled Gene on the street level. Willie had said to his friend, "I need you to bring Gene to the meeting, because I want to be able to tell him that if anything happens to my nephew, that's gonna be on your head."

Uncle Willie was—and still is—very powerful in Harlem. He took me there that night personally in my own car, and his people were surrounding us throughout the entire club, and they were all strapped.

All I could hear was *The Godfather* movie theme playing in my head as we sat down at the table. It was me, Willie, Joseph from Brooklyn, one of Nicky Barnes's longtime friends, Country, and Gene.

Willie started out: "Okay, Gene, I called this truce because I don't want my nephew, in Harlem or anywhere, feeling like he can't go out without looking over his shoulder. I just want to know straight-out: Do you have a contract, or anything, out there on my nephew? Because this boy right here, I'll die for him, and if this is where we're gonna do it, we're gonna do it now, or we gonna call a truce, so he can be on his way and do what he gotta do and end all this bullshit. We need to bring this to peace. Do he owe you anything?"

And Gene said, "No, man, let me tell y'all something right now. I love this boy like he's my son. I took him in like he was my son, and I did everything I could to build his career like he's my son."

Willie countered with the most obvious question: "Then why don't he have no money? This boy here don't have no money. He had to start all over. Why he ain't got his money?"

Well, there it was, all out in the open.

Gene's reply wasn't very reassuring: "Man, I don't know what to say for that. I can tell you this, I have nothing against this boy, and I still to date treat him like he's my son."

Willie responded, "Okay, so you treat him as your son, even after you already took everything from him. What more do you want?"

So Gene again said, "I ain't got nothing to say about that. It's something we'll have to deal with in court, but I can assure you: I have nothing against him, I have nothing on him, and we have no business. So I'm moving on, and I can assure you nothing's gonna happen to him, nothing at all." Looking back on this scene now, it's a little chilling that I had to enlist one Harlem gangster to keep another from making me fear for my life, especially when I was the one who got *ripped off.*

Thankfully, Harlem and all its major gangsters—who I had provided with a soundtrack over the past few years—had my back, and I think Gene knew that he was boxed into a corner. We all shook hands, and Willie took me out of there. Gene went his way, we went our way, and from then on, we handled matters in the courts, because Gene saw real quick that his cash flow had dried up after I left. Amazingly, I eventually wound up having to settle Gene's suit to get his hands out of my pocket completely. I had to agree to pay him 5 percent of everything I would make over the next couple of years because of the slave agreements he'd had me sign as a teenager when I had no idea what I was giving away. Unfortunately for Gene, karma would come back to haunt him big time.

With Gene out of my life, I felt free for the first time, and heading into the 1990s, I immediately started to see a rapid uptick in my income, because this time around everything was being paid directly to me, in my name. That meant that I was able to buy my family the townhouse with the elevator we'd been renting in Teaneck. It was in a nice gated community where my neighbors were Giants football players and fellow recording stars like Keith Sweat, who around this time introduced me to my next manager. I was getting job after job after job, including both the Jane Child and Keith Sweat "Make You Sweat" remixes, and finally starting to reclaim my professional name the only way I knew how: by making hits.

With Guy, I also had the honor that year of recording the title track for *New Jack City*, Mario Van Peebles's hit movie that came out in the spring of 1991. Given that the film was titled after the sound I was popularizing with my productions and Guy, it was a highlight for me to see my music connected with such a groundbreaking gangster movie. I knew they had to put something from me in there: You couldn't really put that New Jack stamp on the film without it. That soundtrack almost feels like a celebration of the mainstream crossover my sound was preparing to make heading into the next decade.

I had some more luck producing Hi-Five's first Billboard R&B Top 10 hit with "I Just Can't Handle It," but I spent the better part of 1990 completing work on *The Future*, Guy's second album and our first album post–Gene Griffin. For me, that record marked a creative triumph, with my name properly acknowledged as writer and producer, and without Gene riding my credit coattails. The sad part for me was that it cost an arm and a leg to get Guy out of their contracts with Gene, but I was grateful to have the album as a creative outlet. Really, it was therapeutic: If you listen, there are a lot of references to Gene throughout the record, where we were all just getting our frustrations out on tape. Unfortunately, Aaron became so depressed about the whole situation that he only sang on about half the record.

Going through the split with Gene was like going through a breakup with a girl, for all of us, and you can hear that on that album also. We talked about the relationship in our songs, how we got robbed, and how this happened and that happened. But we did make our love songs, too: "Wanna Get With U" and "Let's Chill," which went to numbers four and three on the Billboard Hot R&B/Hip-Hop Songs Chart; "Do Me Right," the biggest hit, which peaked at number two, and "D-O-G Me Out," our fourth single to crack the Top 10, at number eight.

But even as our records climbed the charts, there were internal problems in the group beyond just our financial frustrations owing to Gene. I was beginning to sense a growing jealousy from Aaron and Damion, who seemed to get envious any time I got individual press from producing this hip-hop star or that R&B singer. It was starting to feel toxic, though maybe lessened by the fact that, out on tour, there was plenty of female love to go around for all the guys in the group, even as our love for one another was starting to disintegrate.

Thankfully, fans and music critics alike took a shine to *The Future*, with the *L.A. Times* praising both Guy and me individually in a 1991 feature in which the paper reported that "Riley is both the leader of Guy and the architect of the new jack swing sound. At 24, this soft-spoken New Yorker is a veteran of the recording studio . . . One of Riley's strengths is knowing when to intercede and when to hang back and let his collaborators do their own thing. With Guy, this method allows the voices of brothers and co-members Aaron and Damion Hall to lift *The Future* out of the dance-music record bins to the sanctified level of soul music." I was so proud when we hit number one on the Billboard R&B/Hip-Hop Albums Chart. It was a monumental achievement that I knew in my heart marked the group reaching its commercial peak.

◆ ◆ ◆ ◆ ◆

We were out on the road through the end of 1990, and though I loved entertaining the tens of thousands of fans who were now coming out to see us, after a while I got tired of it, naturally being more of a studio fixture. The night that first drove me over the edge had come the previous summer, in July 1989, when we were opening for New Edition. That's when I'd lost one of my best friends from childhood,

Anthony Bee, to what everyone thought was a beef between the New Edition road crew and ours. How it all started is still beyond me to this day, but here's what I know: Kicking off the air of tension that night, the start of the show, which was in Greensboro, North Carolina, got pushed back because New Edition was traveling with a big production, and I believe their buses arrived late.

Then, to add insult to injury, as Guy was still performing, New Edition's production manager came out on stage behind us and started setting up the instruments for their upcoming set. That is simply the biggest slap in the face you can give another band on the same bill with you, and it is considered a *major* sign of disrespect, which it clearly was on the production manager's part. Anthony, who was a member of our road crew, came over and said, "No man, you can't set up while we're still on stage."

But the production manager started claiming, "We aren't setting up on the stage," and they got into an altercation. Our road manager then pushed the production manager off the stage—a ten-foot fall. He got up, went and told the whole New Edition road crew what had happened it, and it was on.

Our show ended abruptly, during "Piece of My Love," when our security team could see things were quickly getting out of hand backstage. They led us off stage in the middle of the song for our safety. I could hear right away from backstage that the audience wasn't happy about that, which threw more fuel on the fire. For our part, we were ushered quickly out of the venue and onto the bus, setting off for the next gig, in Pittsburgh. Sadly, the grudges followed us there. A melee broke out during that show and amid the scuffle, someone pulled out a gun. Anthony was shot multiple times in the back and died at the scene.

It was senseless. Anthony Bee was someone I had looked up to like a big brother or father figure, and he'd kind of guided me through the streets and eventually got me off them because he wanted to see me make it doing music. After that, I'd always kept him close, including by taking him out on the road with us. So in a way, I felt some personal responsibility for his death. It is still the most devastating thing that has ever happened to me in the music industry, and it threw me for a loop. No one else from Guy knew Anthony: He was always known on the road as "Teddy's big brother." That's how close we were regarded by others. When he was shot, I had to take a step back and say to myself, "This is *not* what I signed up for."

That kind of danger is why, even after the truce with Gene, I had security with me everywhere I went. At home, I had a round-the-clock detail to make sure our family was protected, with guys taking shifts, then sleeping on the bottom floor of my house. It was like that for two or three years. In the course of gaining my freedom, I had lost a lot, and even though the security helped make me feel like I was safe so I could focus on my career, the experience of losing my friend made me feel like I needed to get out of the group, at least for a short while. I didn't think it was going to be permanent, but a phone call from the King of Pop changed all that.

I had signed a production deal with MCA Records that took advantage of both my skill at producing hit records and my instinct for breaking new talent. It was a perfect marriage that allowed me to feel some stability for the first time in my life. The MCA Records Group chairman, Al Teller, told journalist Patrick Goldstein that "this is a very important deal for us. Teddy is one of the special ones. We've already been Teddy's artistic home, but this gives us a broader relationship with one of the most creative people in the music business today."

CHAPTER TWELVE

"This Is Michael Jackson. Is Teddy There?"

"Teddy Riley is just incredible. He is also innovative. I love working with him. He's one of my favorites. As a human being, he is one of my dearest people in the world. He's just a really friendly guy."

—MICHAEL JACKSON, SINGER, SONGWRITER, AND PERFORMER

I'd first gotten the call to work with Michael Jackson from Michael's manager, who called my then-manager, Harvey Austin, and said, "Michael would like to talk to Teddy about working together." Michael himself then hopped on the phone with Harvey, who, in his Wolfman

Jack voice, said, "Hold on a minute, I got Teddy right here for you." He put me on the line and history was made. I remember being so nervous because the first word out of Michael's mouth was "Teddy . . ."

I'm sure I sounded like his number one fan even though I was trying to be cool. I said, "Hey Michael," like I already knew him.

He got down to business: "Are you here?" he asked, meaning in LA, but I was back in New York, so I said, "No, was I supposed to be there?"

He replied, in his signature gentle voice, "Yes, you're supposed to be here working with me. We're working on the record together."

I remember sitting there in Harvey's office in a daze, flabbergasted. Michael started asking me a bunch of questions about music and what I was working on at that moment. Then he surprised me by asking, "Is it for me?"

Trying not to sound too eager, I said, "No, I'm actually working on a bunch of things."

Soon enough, he cut to the chase and asked, "Well, can you be here this Saturday?"

Even in the moment, I couldn't believe my reply: "Oh, no, I can't be there *this* Saturday, but I can be there the following Saturday."

Now, you might think that after having Michael Jackson ask me to come out to California and work for him, I'd have been on the first plane out. But the truth was, as I told him, "I'm very excited about coming to be there with you, but I also want to be prepared. I want to be prepared for you because I want to make sure that I have something that will blow your mind."

It turns out this was actually the second time Michael had reached out to me. When I got to LA, I was horrified to discover my now ex-manager Gene Griffin had blocked him when I could have been on the *Bad* album.

Michael and I were in the studio one day when he asked me, "Do you still work with a bald-headed guy?"

I was confused: "A bald-headed guy?"

And he said again, "Yeah, a bald-headed guy who said he was your manager. He was mean. He was a mean guy, and basically messed up your being on the *Bad* album."

Well, when I heard that, my jaw dropped, and Michael could plainly see I was shocked when I asked him, "Oh really?"

It turned out that Quincy Jones had passed on my contact information, including Gene's number, to Michael, who in turn called Gene, and Gene killed it for me.

My eyes went even wider when Michael continued, "Yeah, when I came up with *Bad*, I had you in mind."

More than making me angry, though, after everything I'd already been through with Gene, the news disappointed me. But I was not bitter. I was determined to make a new mark on my own trajectory and, in the process, put all that disappointment in the past. Michael was part of the plan. So many people loved my music, and I would have been able to shine working with Michael on *Bad*. But now, here, four years later, I knew this was my shot at superstardom, and I wasn't going to let anything stand in the way of that, especially not the ghost of Gene. Michael seemed to agree.

"Well, everything happens for a reason," he said. "You're now on the *Dangerous* album, and we're going to really, really shock the world!"

During our initial phone call, I'd told Michael that I had one more concert to do with Guy, where I planned to announce my departure. That also helped buy me the time I needed that week to put together the demos for what would become "Dangerous," the title track to the album. He'd given me some amazing coaching on that call, pumping my ambitions up to the moon with his declaration: "We're going to make a smash. We're going to take it to the sky and reach nothing less than great! I want you to hurt me!"

That stopped me for a second before I replied, "Hurt you?" And oh how he started laughing.

Michael was a great coach, and I was happy to be playing on Team Jackson, the most coveted production spot in the music business. I spent most of that next week with my head buried in making tracks. I actually had three studios running at the same time that week with three engineers working round the clock, because I was also working on the Jane Child remix, a track by Guy, "Why You Wanna D-O-G Me Out?," and the mix of "Make You Sweat" by Keith Sweat.

Despite all that work and the career-making call from Michael, I still had so many negative things coming at me. There was not only the fallout from the split with Gene, but also internal problems within the Guy camp that were long-standing. After our live shows, rather than hitting the after-parties, I'd almost always take refuge from the spotlight in the studio. Aaron and Damion would give me a hard time about not being part of that scene, but I really had to put my foot down because my production career was bringing in more money for me than being in Guy.

The call from Michael proved to be the final nail in the group's coffin. At the time, it seemed to me that rather than being excited, Aaron and Damion were jealous, and it finally got so heated that they told me I had to choose between Michael and the group. I actually announced on stage at Madison Square Garden that I was leaving the group, news that was received by an arena's worth of resounding boos—ironically one of the very few times we were ever booed on stage. Even still, I have to admit, it gave me a huge breath of fresh air when it was finally out in the open. My plan was to focus full-time on producing, and the opportunity to work full-time with Michael Jackson was more than an offer I couldn't refuse. Truthfully, it was the escape I'd been praying for.

There would be one more bit of drama with Guy later when I showed up to rehearsal while Aaron and Damion were auditioning new backup singers, one of whom happened to be Chauncey Hannibal, who would later become a member of Blackstreet. It all went down at Rocket Rehearsal Studios on Eleventh Avenue in New York City. I was there just to listen to the auditions and then had to get on to the studio, but while I was at Rocket, someone asked me if I was going to Damion's birthday party after the rehearsal. I said, "No, I can't go, man. I've got to work on these Michael Jackson records."

The party took place that night at the Mirage. I was at the studio, making the track for "Blood on the Dance Floor," which proved sadly ironic when I got a call from one of my security guys, telling me, "One of Damion's bodyguards got shot and killed on the dance floor." After that, I knew I needed some time away from the craziness that had begun to consume the world of Guy, especially just coming off the danger and drama with Gene.

We tried to put the group back together several times after that, but the dynamics never changed.

I was lucky throughout my come-up to have street guys who humbled me and kept me grounded because they wanted to see me win. Ironically, Guy worked better when Gene was managing the group, because everyone was afraid to go off the deep end and get on his bad side.

So anyway, there was *a lot* going on during that week leading up to me heading out to California to work with Michael. My savior in allowing me to make my deadline was actually Q-Tip of A Tribe Called Quest, who let me use his studio to do the preproduction for "Remember the Time" and other tracks I was preparing for Michael.

Tip had a residency at Soundtracks Studio, and it was in an incredibly small, compact room where he made his beats. I kind of felt bad because I was tapping into his time in the studio. But when I told him what it was for, he said, "Hell yeah, man, you can take it, no worries. And if you got anything for me to do on the record, call me," and that was it. I went in and created the tracks for "Remember the Time," "Blood on the Dance Floor," "Joy," "She Drives Me Wild," and more.

I think I ended up doing fifty-plus tracks that week. Along with the inspiration from Michael, I had another secret weapon in the form of a beautiful actress named Salli Richardson, who was in the studio with me that entire week while I was creating. I'm not the type of guy that needs four or five girls in the studio with me. All I need is one, and it doesn't even need to be sexual—that week, the mere look in Salli's eye could give me crazy musical inspiration. Not just my muse, she was also a close friend who took care of me, who made sure that I ate and had everything I needed to create around the clock. Salli was actually the one who inspired me to write "Remember the Time," which would become one of the album's biggest worldwide hits.

As compact as that room at Soundtracks was, I had an enormous setup that was just off the wall: I used an MPC3000 with an Akai S-900 and 950 samplers, the Akai S-3000 sampler, and my Roland S-90 synthesizer. Everything was cutting edge: I had the D-90, which gave me the beautiful strings on "Remember the Time," along with a D-550 and a D-50, and then a lot of what we called outboard gear, additional music gear used to record with. The day I laid down that song, there were a bunch of fantasies I'd told Salli about, one of which was making love in an elevator, and afterward she made that fantasy come true.

Once we made that one come true, I went immediately into the studio and made that beat, the soundtrack to the fantasy. I was on a musical high when I wrote that song. I was on another one entirely when I wrapped up that week of preproduction and flew first-class to LA to meet Michael.

◆ ◆ ◆ ◆ ◆

When I landed in California, I went straight to Neverland Ranch, north of Santa Barbara, and stayed out there with Michael for a few days while his people were getting things ready at Larrabee, a studio in LA. I was flown from the airport to Michael's ranch on his very own helicopter—my first time ever flying in one.

From the air, Neverland was an incredible sight: It ran on for as far as the eye could see. When we landed, we got into a golf cart that looked like a Mercedes, and the roads to the actual house were straight out of *The Wizard of Oz*—it was literally "Follow the yellow brick road." Being there was like going to an amusement park.

When we arrived at the house, I first met one of Michael's security people. She told me, "Mr. Jackson would like you to wait for him in here," and walked me into a room where all his trophies were displayed: platinum and multiplatinum records, Grammy Awards, humanitarian honors. Funnily enough, what really caught my eye was a chess set, because I played chess. This set had gold and platinum pieces—I was so in awe of that.

I touched a couple of those chess pieces, just to see if they were real gold and platinum, and they were heavy. I was so dazzled by this chess set, I did not realize that Michael had entered the room and snuck up behind me. When he touched my shoulder, I jumped because I was so surprised, and then fell to the ground. He just laughed and laughed and laughed—he was dying laughing. He'd nearly scared me to death, I was so shocked, but I had to keep my cool. He offered me his hand, helped me up off the floor, and said, "It's good to see you and good to meet you, finally. There's so much I want to talk to you about."

Michael wanted to spend some time getting to know me before we dove headlong into the next year of record making. He told me, "I want to spend the whole day talking about music and life," and that's what we did. First, we talked about life, things we loved, my family and children, and then he turned the conversation toward music, asking me, "So what gives you the inspiration to make the music that you make?"

I told him there were so many things that inspired me, but the most important thing was, "I can only get the blessing from God."

Michael and I both shared a deep faith. We got into a very deep conversation about the music that we loved, which legends had inspired us to make our own music. Naturally I told him, "Well, you were one of my inspirations, and Stevie Wonder, James Brown, Marvin Gaye, and Prince." The whole time Michael was sitting there, nodding along, but he suddenly seemed to withdraw when I mentioned Prince. I guess the rumor about those two having a professional rivalry had some truth to it.

Then he said, "I want to show you a tape of me performing at one of James Brown's concerts." It just so happens that years later that tape surfaced on YouTube. It shows Michael at James's concert, and James calling Michael up on stage to dance. But that's an edited version. In the uncut video Michael showed me that day, he says, "Prince is in the audience," and then Prince comes up on stage, too, and let's just say it doesn't go well because Michael basically upstages him. That, incidentally, was the only time in both their careers that they agreed to appear on stage together.

After watching that video, Michael and I continued talking. I mentioned John P. Kee, and he stopped me again, asking, "Who's John P. Kee?"

I thought that was a cool moment: I had the privilege of introducing Michael Jackson to a new artist, explaining to him, "John P. Kee is a gospel singer that a lot of singers get their style from, and a lot of urban R&B singers follow his lead."

He next asked me, "What's the funkiest song that you really like out there?" My answer was basically all of James Brown's songs, and he said, "Me too. James Brown is like a father to me."

Then, he turned the topic to my music and began telling me about his favorite songs that I'd made and what he would like to do with the music we were going to make together. At that point, I said, "Michael, all that you're saying you'd like to do, I think I have it."

We spent a total of two days together, kicking it like that before we ever got to the studio. He also showed me around Neverland. He had a full-on zoo with animals from all around the world: an elephant named Gypsy, a boa constrictor, chimpanzees, parrots, flamingos, even lions. They all knew Michael, too, in one way or another, and he introduced me to all of them. It was a trip, because he could get a lion to be friendly. He would talk to them and say, "This is Teddy. He's my new friend." He even introduced me to Bubbles! That was his favorite chimp, who he used to take on outings and even on tour. Bubbles was very friendly to me; he came to hang out in the studio one time, and it was as if he felt Michael's heart, and who Michael loved, and showed me love in turn. In fact, Michael gave Bubbles's son, Ripley, when he was still a baby chimp to me as a gift. He wanted Bubbles to see who his son was going to, and I remember holding Ripley in my arms, and when he hugged me, he didn't want to let me go. That's when Bubbles reacted happily and excitedly, like "Wow, that's his new parent." Unfortunately, I couldn't take him back to Virginia Beach because they had a law against bringing wild animals home and domesticating them as pets. It really saddened me that I wasn't able to bring Ripley home and raise him there.

I was in awe of *everything*. I spent the night in the guesthouse, which had at least ten master suites, and each suite had Moonwalker linen and big-screen TVs mounted on the walls. Those were the days when only extremely rich people could afford flat-screen televisions with every cable channel you could imagine. It was amazing.

CHAPTER THIRTEEN

Dangerous

"Teddy Riley, you're a genius!"
—MICHAEL JACKSON, 1993 GRAMMY AWARDS

There was so much freedom flowing through my life and music when I was working with Michael. He possessed this beautiful presence in the studio, both as a musical genius and as a person, which was constantly inspiring. He was truly a special kind of star: I'd been discovering and shaping stars my whole career, but recording with Michael wasn't just working on a whole other level—it was like operating in a whole other universe. He was the biggest star in the world and could have picked any producer in the business to work with . . . and he chose me. I knew I had to deliver the strongest songs of my career.

The day after I'd had that initial call from Michael, I'd gone out and bought myself my first Ferrari, a kind of a bonus I gave myself for getting the gig. I had the dealer deliver it from North Carolina to

California because Michael's people had told me, "Listen, we want you to stay here with Michael," and I'd happily replied, "I'll stay as long as you want me to stay!" They actually built me a bedroom *at* Larrabee Studios, in Van Nuys, which was ground zero for the recording of the *Dangerous* album.

Michael asked me how I usually worked, and I'd told him, matter-of-factly, "I usually fall asleep in the studio," so that's why he built me the bedroom. First, he booked me into a suite of my own at a nearby hotel while his people were getting Larrabee ready for our arrival. In one week, they dressed the studio and built my bedroom. That's how Michael was: Your wish was his command if it made you more comfortable while working. Personally, his generosity was endless as well.

By then, I was very wealthy, so I had all my stuff: I had three racks of S-3000s, S-950s, and 900s, about four MPC-3000s and MPC-60s, and I had Logic on an Otari computer. In fact, I had bought seven Otari computers because they would go out on you, and I didn't want that to happen with me and Michael. Once we were in California, Michael gave us an advance of around $100,000 for studio expenses, so I was like, "Wow, okay, we're going to go get the right equipment!" I had a guy make me a rack system that connected everything through MIDI, and man, it was just crazy.

Not long after we'd started production in principle on the album, Michael left for a ten-day trip to Switzerland. We'd been working nonstop for four months, so I thought, *Great! I'm going to take a quick vacation home to see my family and children.*

When I mentioned that, he said, "No, I need you there at the studio. Nobody will be able to work without you there."

I said, "Okay, but I miss my family."

His reply: "Okay, we'll bring your family to California. I will make sure everybody gets here, but I need you not to leave, Teddy. Please stay."

Of course I agreed to stay, and Michael flew my friends and family out and rented them cars to get around. Everyone visited for a week, except my daughter, Deja, who was now two years old. She came, too, but then stayed and never went back. When she met Michael, she fell in love.

I spent every day and night with him in the studio for almost a year and a half, and I can tell you I never saw *anything* inappropriate happen between Michael and young children. I even trusted him with my own, because Deja was in the studio with Michael and me every day, along with her childhood best friend, Brandon Howard, the future singer, songwriter, and producer. They'd play games, they'd watch movies—nothing more. A year later, after Michael was first accused, I even told him, "Listen, if you need me there, I'll come." Once during that whole nightmare, I did privately fly out there to spend time with Michael.

The media spotlight on him was so intense during the scandal, with reporters and paparazzi following him everywhere, camped out at every exit of any building he ever entered, that we had a whole spy-like route to sneak me into the hotel where he was staying, where we talked for hours and hours. I think at that point, he just needed his friends close by because for the first time in his life, he was being treated differently by the public. But the media attention was nothing new. Back when we were working together, the paparazzi were chasing him everywhere, too, which helps explain why we stayed locked down in the studio most of the time I was out there.

Working on *Dangerous* was a great time in my life, because I was free of everything. I wound up spending fifteen months in California, working day and night in the studio with Michael and his engineer, Bruce Swedien, making music. Michael eventually built a bedroom for himself in the studio as well, plus a game room and two kitchens—one for me and one for him. He even brought his personal chef down from Neverland, a master at cooking organic Indian food. That's when I began my lifelong love affair with Indian food, but he could make anything else we wanted too. And every Tuesday or Wednesday, we'd order Popeye's chicken because Michael loved their butter biscuits. So we had everything we needed at our disposal right there at the studio, which meant we never had to leave and could keep working around the clock.

After Michael got back from his trip to Europe, Bruce Swedien had jokingly admonished him that his absence was "holding up the project," so that became the slogan for the entire album's recording: "NO HOLDING UP THE PROJECT!" We even printed up signs that were hung on the doors to everyone's bedrooms, the lounge and the kitchens, and everywhere else throughout the studio. It became an inside joke among the studio staff, because we had so much musical momentum going.

The greatest compliment Michael paid me during the entirety of our time working together came the very first day at Larrabee. I was letting him hear what I'd been working on for him ahead of my arrival in California. The first track I played him, out of the fifty or more I'd prepared, was "Blood on the Dance Floor." The whole time he was listening I could see he was trying to keep his cool, but he was already thinking up the words to the song in his mind. (And we did end up recording that track.) But then he heard the next three tracks, and with each, said, "Keep going, keep going." I then played him "Joy." He said, simply, "This is not me." ("Joy" eventually went to Blackstreet.)

Then we got to the fifth track, which was "Remember the Time," and that was it. That was the track he couldn't help but dance to while he was listening. But then, abruptly, he stopped everything—his dancing, the music itself—and pulled me to the back of the room, away from everyone else. Truthfully, I didn't know if I was going to get fired or what. He just asked me, "What were those chords?" and it turned out to be one of the greatest compliments he could have ever paid me because he said, "The chords that you used are different from the chords that I would regularly use in my music. Everything I play is Major, or straight Minor, or maybe a 7th." But I was using augmented 9s and was all into New Jack Swing chords, which, for some context, were basically inspired by church chords, though I would put them in progressions and relate them to how I play, with added notes and the goal of basically having people say, "I like that chord, but I have no idea what he's playing there . . ." I just played them differently than everybody else. Michael actually paid me the high compliment of telling me I'd taught him something new. That was something I never expected to hear from a musician of his experience and depth, and the moment remains a highlight of my career.

I had brought Michael something unorthodox and unexpected. He actually called up Emmanuel Lewis, the young actor who played the title character on the 1980s sitcom *Webster*, to come down and give him a second opinion. Remember, Michael was trying to modernize his sound to tap into the current generation of teenagers who were growing up on my New Jack Swing sound, so this was a different direction for him. When Emmanuel got there, Michael had me replay everything in the same order, only this time we got up to ten tracks, and they kept saying, "Play some more." There the both of them were, behind the console, dancing—Michael Jackson and Webster.

It was important to give Michael something that would shock the world, where people just have no choice but to listen and move, where the music's power would be undeniable. He wanted stuff that would hurt you on the dance floor. That's what he would always say, "I need you to hurt me with this record. The mix, I need it to hurt me. I need to be laying on the floor from the kick drum, banging the room out!" That's the one thing about Michael: He loved his music so loud that Bruce Swedien and I had to leave the room sometimes.

Earplugs didn't help, so Bruce would say, "Okay, Michael, I'm going to start the tape up and then leave the room." The opening chords from "Remember the Time" would come on while he was running out, and then as soon as those hard drums kicked in, Michael and Emmanuel Lewis would get down and dance all day right there in the studio, while I was sitting at the console working.

While a lot of the songs we did together for *Dangerous* came out of those demos I'd created prior to arriving in LA, other singles off the album we just made up in the studio together, right there on the spot. One of those was "In the Closet." I remember Michael started humming and beatboxing, which was basically the opening of the song once the beat got going.

I said, "Well, you need a bass in there," and he said, "Well, I don't know what I would do."

So I said, "Alright, do that again with your mouth and I will do something on the piano."

(He would not let me use a synthesizer. "Everything is natural on the piano," he always said.) He started doing the rhythm track again with his mouth, and I started playing along with that bass line, based on a James Brown song, which I just sped up. We were just on fire from there! That was the temperature of that record. Michael then said, "We've got to do another one," which is when we came up with "She Drives Me Wild."

He would always say that our chemistry was almost like when he used to work with Randy, his little brother, who had joined the Jacksons in their later years and also contributed to Michael's breakthrough *Off the Wall* album. "You remind me so much of Randy," he would tell me. "Randy would just come up with these grooves, and sometimes he didn't even know what he had." Michael felt the same way about me, because he would often ask, "Do you know what this is?" while I was playing him something. I'd say, "No, it's a track, it's a track for you," and he'd say, "No, this is *genius*." To hear a universally acknowledged musical genius like Michael Jackson say that about your music, you truly feel like you're moonwalking across the stars.

The album opener, "Jam," was unique because the drums were programmed by Michael, so when we started working, the dynamic was like when Doug E. Fresh already had the drum beat for "The Show." Michael did the vocals, then I said, "Give me the track. I know exactly what I want to do." I gave it Earth, Wind & Fire style, but up-tempo. To finish that one off, we had Heavy D come in to rap on the song.

We had all three Larrabee studios running at once, and we wound up locking up the entire complex for that whole year. Money was no object in Michael's world, and that luxury was wonderful to have as a producer. I didn't ever have to worry about my console settings being disturbed, or microphones being moved around for another session happening in the same room after mine ended, which is typically how it works at a studio that busy. Everything would be exactly as I'd left it when I went to bed the night before. When I woke up, I was that much more focused because I didn't have to deal with the distraction of setting up the board again. It was a beautiful creative continuity that contributed greatly to the magic we were creating inside those rooms.

If I wasn't in that studio, Michael would ask, "Where's Teddy?"—not to say we were codependent, or anything like that, but he was usually in my studio with me working. A very close relationship of trust inevitably develops between artist and producer when you spend that much time with each other, sharing what are often the most vulnerable parts of yourself while writing music together. That trust was a cornerstone of my relationship with Michael, professionally and, in time, personally, because he would confess his innermost thoughts to me, share dreams he had yet to achieve, discuss his private life—women and so forth. No one's going to talk to you in that kind of depth unless they consider you a friend.

We were an unstoppable team, and the more time I spent with Michael Jackson, working alongside a true genius, the better a producer I became. I was very conscious that I was following in the footsteps of Uncle Quincy, already a veteran producer when he'd begun working with Michael on *Off the Wall*, then *Thriller* and *Bad*. For my part, I had to get over being nervous—of being afraid, for instance, to tell Michael during a vocal session, "Your voice is off." That took some time. It was another layer of trust that had to be built up between Michael and me. But we got there. He would listen and never push back if I asked him to do another vocal take, or re-sing a line or a phrase.

The only time he challenged me or anyone on the team, including Bruce, was when we finished with principal recording and had started coming up with preliminary mixes. He was relentless with all the engineers, again using his favorite phrases, saying things like, "I need to be hurt in the studio," or "I need people to hurt me with the sound." He wanted to be blown away by the mixes and kept challenging us to go further, which worked as an effective strategy to pull the best out of us. By that point, we only had two or three weeks left to finalize all the songs for the album before it had to be handed in, and he just had us on this mission: mixing, finishing vocals, everything.

I remember that when we were listening through other cuts while he was trying to decide what should be the first song, I told him, "'Black or White' should be the first single," in part because I was nervous about having one of my songs go out as the first. (Michael had written "Black or White" with the producer Bill Bottrell.)

He agreed: "Okay, I have to make a statement culture-wise with 'Black or White.'" But then he added, "You better not say *no*, Teddy: 'Remember the Time' is the second single."

Even after the album was finished, Michael and I were glued together at the hip. He trusted my input so intuitively by that point that he even wanted me to be present in the marketing meetings with Sony. He wanted me there when he chose the album cover, which was based on a collage that he'd been designing in his bed-room at the studio. Every time he'd added something new, he'd shown it to me to get my take. He wanted me at the meetings when they picked the order of singles. He wanted my input on all kind of little details—for instance, it was my suggestion that Michael put his hair in a ponytail and wear a tight T-shirt for the "In the Closet" video. Things like that.

Michael even tried to sign me to his publishing company. I was already locked up with Zomba, but he said to me, "When you're free, I want to sign you." Word of that must have gotten back up the chain of command at Zomba, because when my contract was up, the company re-signed me with a huge, *huge* advance, knowing Michael was waiting in the wings. Truly, every aspect of being involved with Michael Jackson, professionally and personally, changed my life: both at the time and into the future, with ripple effects like the one I just mentioned. It put me in a club that few record producers ever get to say they've been members of, and I'm proud of that distinc-tion to this day because it will last forever, just like the music we made together. Our work remained banging on the Billboard Top 200 Album Chart for a record 117 weeks and earned me my first Grammy Award, for Best Engineered Album.

Dangerous remains the most successful album of my career as a producer, selling over 35 million copies worldwide, hitting number one in the U.S. and numerous other countries around the world. Meanwhile, "Remember the Time" made number one on the Hot R&B Singles Chart and number three on the Hot 100. Years later, *Vibe* magazine would reflect on the history Michael and I made together with that record: "Before *Dangerous*'s 'Remember the Time,' New Jack Swing had enjoyed a hugely successful run as America's coolest trend-setting youthful soundtrack. Everyone it seems wanted that Teddy Riley magic, including the biggest entertainer on the planet—Michael Jackson . . . 'Remember the Time' exploded out of the speakers . . . From its visuals to its gospel-rooted groove, [the song] was unapologetically black . . . The track's overall reach was clear as it hit the top 10 in more than 11 countries. Jackson had taken Riley's New Jack Swing to new global heights making the newest era of rhythm and blues into the go-to pop sound."

CHAPTER FOURTEEN

Future Studios, Virginia Beach, VA

"Future Recording was just amazing, and it was just so comfortable. It was constant—he was at the studio for the most part. He brought the heat, and the rest is fucking history. When I heard 'Two Can Play That Game,' I had to have that song! Teddy has this work ethic. He tends not to go home—he'll be in the studio day in and day out, then take five hours and go to sleep. But he also had his room at the studio where he'd go take a nap. We'd be vibing and writing, then he'd get up, come back and listen to what we had, and start a new track to it. Teddy Riley is a mastermind. We weren't just trying to make hit records. We were trying to make music that would last, and I'm totally grateful that the music we made has lasted generation after generation after generation, because that's what we were trying to make music for."

—BOBBY BROWN, SINGER, SONGWRITER, AND RAPPER

"I think he was probably the biggest help for me in my career. I'd go down there for the next three years, every school break and summer, from age fourteen through seventeen. Whenever I got the opportunity to sit next to him at the console, I was like a little hawk, watching Teddy create. He was just in the zone, and when he was, I'd never seen anything like it. Teddy was a daring, fearless producer; he had an imagination that was pretty out of this world, and he proved it time and time again."

—RODNEY JERKINS, PRODUCER AND RAPPER

Financially, my work on *Dangerous* was a lifesaver, along with the large advance MCA gave me for my new state-of-the-art production deal, because when I'd started working with Michael, I was still paying off a lot of debts that were left to me by Gene. By the completion of *Dangerous*, I was debt-free and feeling financially safe for the first time in my life.

In 1991, I decided to relocate full-time to Virginia Beach to start building my own empire, beginning with the construction—which was already underway—on what would become my very own state-of-the-art recording studio, appropriately titled Future.

I chose to set up shop in Virginia Beach because I was looking to start over and be someplace where there was no music scene. I had traveled there as a teenager on spring break for Freaknik with some friends of mine: Azie "AZ" Faison, Alpo Martinez, and Rich

Porter. (The film *Paid in Full* is based on their street exploits.) I went to school with Rich at Martin Luther King High School, and those three actually chartered a bus for us, and guys from around the hood chipped in to bring their girls. Well, when I'd gone down there years earlier, I had told my then-girlfriend, "This is the place where I want to come and live," because it was far enough removed from New York but still near enough to commute when I needed to, as I still did a lot of business in the city.

I knew I could move my family into a nice house and still afford to build and operate my own studio. I'd already bought my mother a home in South Carolina. That was a dream come true for both of us: She'd picked out the house she wanted, and I'd paid for it in cash—that's something I'd always wanted to do for my mom. She still has that house today. As for mine, since I'm a homebody and mostly in the studio, I wanted to design a house that would be my sanctuary away from everything: It was on the beach, had a pool, and I could see the ocean from every view.

Because I had always had Gene's hands in my pockets, I'd never truly been able to enjoy success and the freedom of having my own money before. Now, I felt I'd earned that. I had a beautiful collection of cars, but my most prized possession was the recording studio that had been under construction while I was off working with Michael and was now near completion. Cars and bling were one thing; this was about investing in myself. The nice thing was that I owned it outright, no mortgage.

Initially, I had my studio in the house, but then we'd found a building owned by a wildlife photographer who was selling the property so he could move back to his homeland in Africa. We got the building for a steal, at $290,000 cash. It was five thousand square feet, and once I bought it, we immediately gutted some of the rooms and started rebuilding. I actually had to have it gutted twice before we got it right, because the contractor who worked on the floor plan while I was in LA did a terrible job and then, while I was still out there working with Michael, a second team had come in and done an equally awful job.

The specifications of a recording studio's design are unique compared to most buildings because you're not talking about traditional architecture, where most considerations are cosmetic or functional in basic ways. Of course, I wanted my studio to look beautiful, but its sonic architecture was more important. Each room had to have the right sound—for instance, the live room where drums would be recorded—so finally, near the end of my work with Michael, after I'd developed such a solid relationship with the team that ran Larrabee Sound Studios, I hired them to come in and do the job right.

Essentially, I had them build me a replica of the studio I'd been working in for the past two years with Michael, which I found so inspiring. They did the best possible job: I now had every piece of gear I'd been working with during *Dangerous* in my own studio, right down to the console, which was a beautiful SSL 4000 E Series with a Commodore J Computer. The sound of Blackstreet, the new band

I'd formed, was that console. It was so special; everything that came through that console had a warmth you don't typically get from the computer sound or typical interfaces made today. Nothing sounds like the SSL or the Neve or the Ufonics, those real consoles that are analog. There's nothing coming straight out of a computer that can compare to that at all.

What was most enjoyable was being able drive back and forth to the studio, or drive not straight to the studio but to the Virginia Beach strip, just to get ideas in my head. I would get up, have breakfast with the family—my wife, Donna, would make the best French toast—and see my children off to school. Then I'd drive from the house to the boardwalk in one of my Ferraris or my Porsche and take a stroll on the beach to see the ocean and stoke my creative fires for the day. I would walk down to isolated parts of the beach, sit and come up with song ideas, then make my way to the studio. It would give me a whole breath of fresh air and new creativity to come up with music. Most times I traveled with my security, but these times, when I could just drive without being accosted by fans for autographs, I left my security behind so I could have my peace.

◆ ◆ ◆ ◆ ◆

One of the first big projects I recorded at Future Recording Studios was *Bobby*—Bobby Brown's follow-up to the now legendary *Don't Be Cruel* LP. This time out he wanted to go big on New Jack Swing, expanding on the energy and direction of "My Prerogative," and I couldn't wait to get started. As a bonus, Bobby was not only one of the biggest R&B stars in the world at that point but he was also becoming one of the biggest stars *period* because he'd married Whitney Houston in 1992.

When I got word that she was coming down with him to Virginia Beach, the hairs stood up on my arm. I knew just meeting Whitney was going to be fun, but when I found out I was going to be producing a duet she was doing with Bobby, "Something in Common," which would become a Top 20 hit in the U.S. and U.K., I felt like we were getting ready to make another little piece of music history, and certainly make history for Future Studios. What really impressed me about Whitney in the studio was that she came so prepared that she basically got in and got out. When you said you were "producing Whitney Houston," you had to know what you were talking about, because in truth Whitney produced herself. She would give the producer the idea from when she hit a vocal run or riff or melody, and I was adapting to her. It gave me even more insight and inspiration to then say, "Okay, Whitney, can you take it here?" Whitney was more like her own vocal producer, even though I was sitting behind the console recording her. I was just lending my insight instead of telling her exactly how to sing the notes that she owned.

That studio was producing hits around the clock once we were up and running. The first self-titled Blackstreet album came through my SSL next, and so many producers who would become platinum successes in their own right got their start on that board, from the Neptunes' Pharrell Williams and Chad Hugo to Rodney Jerkins, Hannon Lane (who works with Timbaland), Danjahandz, Nottz and Bink Dog, and beyond. I did Wreckx-n-Effect's *Hard or Smooth* album on that console too. It was a blast collaborating with my brother, Markell, who was one of the flagship members of the group. The record was actually a pilot project for the studio because it was the first hit album—it included "Rump Shaker," number two on the Billboard Hot 100 Singles Chart—that I developed at Future. We even shot the video in Virginia Beach. I mentored a lot of aspiring producers during the 1990s at Future, which led me to discover Pharrell Williams and Chad Hugo.

When I get an idea, even before I demo it instrumentally, I begin by making sounds with my mouth. I sound out everything before I make the music, always. Pharrell got that technique from me, and so did Rodney Jerkins. They make music with their mouths first, and then they go in the studio. I do it on my phone now: I use a little multitrack machine app. I'll be making rhythms into it, and when people ask, "What are you doing?" I always tell them, "I'm making rhythms that don't go together. That's how it works."

I was looking for artists who were innovative. I was on the hunt for diamonds in the rough who had swag but didn't know the type of swag they had. Take the song "Rump Shaker." I did a guest rap on it and gave Pharrell the opportunity to write it. That created the swag of Pharrell and helped create the next level of swag in Teddy Riley. It also helped create the next direction for Wreckx-n-Effect, because we didn't quite know where we were going with the new album after making the first one, with the anthem "New Jack Swing." Discovering and teaching Pharrell remains one of my proudest moments as a mentor.

With Pharrell, I feel like what I passed on to him, he's still doing today: locking himself down in the studio, keeping away from the drama, and staying on the creative cutting edge. I was just passing down that work ethic so that one day he and the others I mentored could themselves discover and mentor new Pharrells, new Teddys, and new Timbalands. We're the ones that mold and shape the new hit-makers, so it's like a family tree. In that spirit, I was mentoring a new generation of producers at Future.

Another discovery was an especially talented thirteen-year-old by the name of Rodney Jerkins, who showed up one morning in the parking lot after driving all night with his dad from New Jersey to meet me. It was flattering when he told me he'd grown up reading about me in *Word Up!* and *Black Beat* magazines, hanging Guy posters on his wall, and modeling his musical dreams on what I'd achieved, similar to the way that, when I was his age, I had based mine on Michael Jackson. Rodney told me my music moved him in a way he couldn't fully explain—that beautiful musical mystery for every listener when they hear something they haven't heard before and it captures their imagination. I was very familiar with that feeling myself, and happy to have transitioned into the role where I was now mentoring the next generation of superstar producers. So as with Pharrell, I took Rodney under my wing and tried to teach him everything I could while working on projects I had signed to my label that were coming out of Future Studios.

Being a producer, you need patience—patience for everything: people, technology failures, anything in the way of obstacles and challenges—and I've applied that lesson to everything in life, including my relationships, my friendships, and my brotherhoods. I don't ever want to be in a situation of turmoil, so I'm the equalizer, the peacemaker, the shrink, the counselor, the student, and, just as importantly, the teacher.

✦ ✦ ✦ ✦ ✦

When I thought it was time, I was proud to be the first to introduce Rodney Jerkins to Michael Jackson. Rodney is like a brother to me, and his father and mother are like godparents to me. I never wanted to manage Rodney. I just wanted to guide him in the right direction, and I think I did that by introducing him to Michael and certain other people in the business, so that he had the right people around him to take him to the next level.

As with other producers I've mentored throughout the years, I'm proud of Rodney's success with stars like Beyoncé, Jennifer Lopez, Lady Gaga, and Justin Bieber. He's an incredible producer, still has his dynasty going, and thanks me to this day for giving him that introduction to Michael—just like Pharrell, who, if it wasn't for me, would not know Jay-Z, and you wouldn't have "Happy." I've always been a facilitator, like Quincy Jones, putting talented people together. I'm grateful to God that I have been at the right place and time so often throughout my career to be a catalyst, and that I am still doing so today. It just always pays itself forward.

This was all possible because the global success of *Dangerous* made me one of the most in-demand producers in the music industry, which meant that business at Future Studios was booming. I had just signed a new high-service production deal with MCA Records, and the New Jack Swing movement was cresting into its next wave. I was getting calls from everyone in the business: Mary J. Blige, Patti LaBelle, even Hammer, who called me up to help him produce what would become his comeback hit, "Pumps and a Bump," shortly after he'd signed with Death Row Records. By that point, Dr. Dre had left the label, but little did I know that our stars would soon shine together on a little song called "No Diggity," which would become one of the biggest hits of the 1990s.

CHAPTER FIFTEEN

Blackstreet
and "No Diggity"

"The brainchild of producer Teddy Riley, Blackstreet was the sound of Riley getting back into the groove of performing, which he hadn't done since his former group Guy broke up. After single-handedly defining the New Jack Swing sound that swept R&B in the early '90s, Riley stretched out musically on his group's four studio albums, the best of which is Another Level.*"*

—ROLLING STONE

Blackstreet. The name came to me from the names of the original members: Chauncey Hannibal, who I had nicknamed Chauncey Black, and Joseph Stonestreet, who would sing lead on "Baby Be Mine," our very first single, from the soundtrack to Chris Rock's movie *CB4*. I took the "Black" from Chauncey and the

"Street" from Joseph, put them together, and Blackstreet was born. It would become my next multiplatinum success story and really mark the beginning of the next post-Guy era in my career.

Looking back on it now, I kick myself in the ass for giving the group's original members credits as writers on all of my Blackstreet songs. Eric Williams did make writing contributions, but they were album cuts, not hits. But in the spirit of trying to take care of my band, I shared too much of my generosity by giving each of the original members—Chauncey, Eric, and David Hollister—3 to 5 percent of the publishing on our biggest albums. They still today have credits and receive royalties from those songs. I also couldn't disagree more with the court's eventual ruling that they had rights to use the band's trademark to tour, while I did not. Blackstreet was 100 percent my creation, from the concept to the casting of its members, all of whom I auditioned and trained in the studio. I taught them everything about how to be professional recording artists, from how to sing the specific parts I wrote for them on our biggest hits to how the music business worked.

Chauncey Hannibal would be the best example of that, because he was a janitor at the studio before I ever gave him a deal. I knew Chauncey was a singer, because I'd first met him a few years earlier when he was auditioning for Guy, though I felt like he wasn't yet developed enough vocally to step into the spotlight. At some point in the early 1990s, he rang me up with the kind of call I got from people all the time: "You got a job over there for me?" When I asked him what was going on, he told me Damion Hall was moving back to New York and he'd been staying with him. So I took mercy and gave him that custodial job at Future Studios. He didn't even have a vehicle, so I let him drive one of the company cars, a nice Jeep Cherokee, that we kept at the studio to ferry artists to and from their hotels and around town when they came in to record there. From there, I found him a new place to stay, and a salary. He became not only the janitor but also the guy who made sure everything was running right at the studio.

Once Future Studios' construction was completed, I would frequently travel back and forth to continue working with Michael Jackson, and while I was gone, Chauncey was becoming a known face around Future. One of the other producers working there began to work with him a little vocally, because he had talent, but he was still rough.

When I finished working with Michael and came back home, Chauncey was still working for me, under my studio manager. I was getting ready to record the Bobby Brown album and needed a demo singer for some of the tracks. I thought that would be my chance to train Chauncey to sing like more of a smooth R&B vocalist, because he didn't have the swag for New Jack Swing. But I wasn't thinking about any kind of new group until one day when Chauncey asked, "Can you build a group around me?"

I said, "Yes, we can," and then he got bolder and asked, "Well, if we're building a group, why don't you be part of it?"

My initial reaction was that I didn't know if I wanted to be part of a group again, but if I did, I had hopes of getting Guy back together, and didn't know if starting up another group would work well for me as far as fans were concerned. I told Chauncey I didn't know if I wanted to be a member, but that I'd develop the group and write and produce the songs with them. I tasked him with finding the other singers, and said, "I'll put something together for you." But it's important to note that Chauncey was in the group as a vocalist, *not* a songwriter. That's because he wasn't a writer. That wasn't his natural gift; his gift was his voice.

By the time Joseph Stonestreet came to audition for the group, I had gotten more involved out of necessity—it had really become my project due to everyone else's inexperience. I had already given Chauncey the stage name "Chauncey Black." Just like a song title rings out to me, and I know it's a keeper, I merged the two singers' names into Blackstreet, and we had our new group's name.

It was during the recording of the *Bobby* album when we developed the Blackstreet sound. Part of it was kind of dumbing down the sound of New Jack Swing and putting more layers of music into it. I also wanted singers in all ranges, because I wanted every singer in Blackstreet to do independent singing on the record, which makes a difference: Everybody could sing on one song together, and anybody could sing a song of their own. I was trying to create a modern-day Temptations or Isley Brothers.

We didn't have that on the first two Guy albums because we

didn't have Auto-Tune back then. I felt certain collaborators of mine had the ear to sing live, but not in the studio, and there's a distinct difference between the two. That's what I had to train Chauncey for, because he wasn't initially great singing in the studio, a vocal skill that developed over time through our working together. Dave Hollister, who would join the group later, was perfect singing in the studio, in the bathtub, singing everywhere, and it was the same with Joseph Stonestreet.

Joseph could actually cover his ears and still be on key, whereas that was hard for Damion and Chauncey—especially Chauncey, who would frequently sing flat. In order to get him to sing on key, I used all kinds of cool producer tricks: For instance, I would actually sing something at a higher key for him, and he would sing it at that higher key, and then I would turn the music down in his headphones so that he could hear what he was singing mostly over the music. He would sing along to himself and just the beat.

I felt so much more pressure working with Blackstreet than I had with Guy because I was in the forefront now. This was *my* group, and my sound was being taken in a different direction. At the same time, the guys didn't have the stage presence we needed. I had to start all over with artist development so that they looked as good as they sang, and everything matched and it wasn't boring like some quartet doing the two-step side by side.

So developing them as a group didn't mean just training them by getting a vocal coach to keep the strength of the stage vocals and harmonies *in* harmony. It also meant putting a choreographer in front of them. Thankfully, because I'd spent the better part of a decade on both sides of that role—as both a producer developing artists and as an artist myself as a member of Guy (and not even counting everything I'd learned working with Michael Jackson), I knew every aspect of what made a superstar.

That made Blackstreet easier to produce than Guy when we started working on the group's self-titled debut album at the end of 1993, and all the work we'd done meant that by the time that first record was set to hit the streets, the group had developed a sound and style all its own.

We had had a little shake-up in the group's lineup, too, namely Joseph Stonestreet's replacement by Dave Hollister, who still sings with me today in Blackstreet 2. But that bump aside, we found immediate success on radio right out of the gate. We had a Top 10 single with "Before I Let You Go," and the album was certified platinum within a year of its release. Maybe the most special moment for me came when we recorded another single off that album, "Joy," which I'd cowritten with Michael Jackson during the *Dangerous* sessions but didn't make it to the album. That was an incredible moment for me, when he gave us that song.

By 1995, I had my sights set on painting a masterpiece with Blackstreet's sophomore album, *Another Level,* and we would hit that new level with what became the group's signature hit, "No Digity," which took the world by storm. I knew the minute my fingers first hit the song's opening piano notes that I had a number one on my hands. It was the same producer's instinct that had told me that even when "Remember the Time" was a demo, it was going to be a huge hit for Michael, or the same for "My Prerogative" and Bobby Brown. But the funny thing is, when I first came up with that hook, I didn't know what to do with it. I got it from the Roland 770 samples, and I remember saying to myself, "You know what? I'm going to save that hit for something special." The perfect opportunity came with "No Diggity."

The part reminded me so much of when a TV show ends, that little cartoon melody they always played at the end of the credits. That's what I was thinking when we recorded the lines, "Shorty get down, good Lord / Baby got 'em open all over town / Strictly biz, she don't play around / Cover much ground / Got game by the pound," insert piano hit, then "Getting paid is her forte . . ." To me, that was my version of what they'd do back in the day, where a comedian would say something, then they would have the sting, that short drum sequence *ba-dum-tss*.

I programmed that whole song on the MPC-60, which I still use to date. (I'm on the MPC renaissance right now.) I knew the record was strong even before we added Dr. Dre's verse, which happened as an afterthought. Dre was initially involved as an unofficial A&R man because he's actually the one who convinced Jimmy Iovine—the head of our label, Interscope—that that song was a hit. Jimmy wasn't really a fan at first of "No Diggity."

Jimmy wanted "Money Can't Buy Me Love" to be the first single, but both Dre and Heavy D told him, "Teddy Riley has a big record on his hands." The promotion guys, when we were all listening to the finished album together for the first time at the Interscope office, weren't fans of the song either. It went back even further than that: I had to agree to sing the first verse myself on the album version because the other Blackstreet members didn't believe in "No Diggity" either, and none of them wanted to be the first voice on the track.

I was adamant. I told Jimmy, "This should be the first single," and I believed in it so much that the president of my company took it upon herself to press up a thousand copies of the single, and she gave them to DJs. That's when momentum started rolling. Dr. Dre heard the song, came to us before the video had been shot, and said to Jimmy, "Tell Teddy that I want to be in the video when he do this joint right here, because I want to be able to dance on this song!"

My response was, "No, if he's gonna do anything, he's gonna give me sixteen bars, because I don't want it to look like he's just in my video." Dre agreed because he believed in the song that much.

So that was the thing about "No Diggity": It was one of those records that I alone believed in and knew was very special. But I was happy to have Dre and Heavy back me up. Heavy had said, "Man, you're breaking the rules with this record." Those are the guys— Heavy D, Dr. Dre, Andre Harrell, Larry Harris, Nelson George, Fab 5 Freddy, and Sway—who, when they say, "That record there!" you listen. And once Jimmy Iovine saw the momentum picking up with the song, he got 100 percent behind it. Jimmy is the type of guy who when he truly believes in something, trust me, it's going all the way to the top.

I was one of Jimmy's favorite people in that era, so with both me and Dre on the same record, it was going *past* number one, and damn right, when it did, I was sitting there wearing my "told you so" smile. I've always found that people don't hear a hit until it slaps them in their face.

Blackstreet had another lineup change before we began work on *Another Level*, with the addition of Eric Williams to the group. Chauncey had first brought him to my attention when they had both come in to audition for background singer spots when Guy was still together. I felt he wasn't ready. Like Chauncey, his voice wasn't yet strong enough.

But by 1995, after I'd helped Chauncey develop into a real R&B singer, I decided to give Eric a shot to replace Dave Hollister. To round out the group, we added another new member in Mark Middleton. Critically and commercially, my A&R choices paid off because our second album sold four million copies and shot all the way to number three on the Billboard Top 200 Album Chart and number one on the Top R&B/Hip-Hop Albums Chart. And thanks to "No Diggity," Blackstreet was honored in 1998 with a win at the Grammy Awards for Best R&B Performance by a Duo or Group with Vocals. After that, Janet Jackson called me up to bring the group into her 1999 duet hit with Ja Rule on "Girlfriend/Boyfriend," which also featured Eve.

♦ ♦ ♦ ♦ ♦

Even with everything I had going on with Blackstreet, my collaboration with Michael Jackson continued to bear fruit, with our song "Ghosts" appearing on the *Addams Family* soundtrack and on Michael's *HIStory* greatest hits album. In 1997, "Blood on the Dance Floor" was released as a worldwide single to promote his remix album of the same title. Though that one didn't do that well in the States, its global chart success reflected just how many new listeners my name was now reaching: UK Singles Chart (number one), Spain Singles Chart (number one), New Zealand Singles Chart (number one), Danish Singles Chart (number one), Swedish, Norwegian, and Finnish Singles charts (number two), and a Top 5 hit in Australia, Germany, Romania, Switzerland, and Ireland. I also found time to work with a young Jay-Z on the million-selling *In My Lifetime Vol. 1*, his second album. The lead single, "The City Is Mine," featured Blackstreet and was a Top 40 hit on the Billboard Hot 100 Singles Chart.

Footnote: We've gotten some heat from fans and the press over the years when the original members of Blackstreet wouldn't reunite for this awards show or that legacy celebration, but that's indicative of how deep my feeling of mistrust went. The truth is: I don't need them to sell out arena shows or pack amphitheaters. I can play the Blackstreet hits with my band BLKRC and we'll sound just like the records did. So if you want to come out and hear those hits, come to my show and we will make you feel like you're right there back in 1996, dancing at your high school prom or wedding or in your college fraternity or sorority while our records are bumping out of the speakers.

I have the loyalty I do among the Blackstreet fans who still come out by the tens of thousands every year to hear me sing these songs, and they even sing them back to me acapella. That's how connected I am to my fans, no matter through which of my groups they discovered my music. At the heart of it all is the bond between Teddy Riley and my listeners. I wrote those songs for *you*, not for the former members of Blackstreet, and these days, at my age and level of success, I don't have the energy anymore to deal with all the jealousy, animosity, negativity, and drama that naturally comes with that kind of reunion. I save my energy for my fans. I love to share nostalgia with them, but I have no more room in my life for the old shit.

When Chauncey showed up at my mother's funeral, after she died in February 2024, and being that his mother was there with him, I opted to be as nice as I've ever been to him. But truthfully, there's not a lot of love lost between us. I felt like telling him, "Yo, I don't really want to deal with you. You're not the guy I know anymore and gave the name Black to. You're not the same guy, and that's why I'll never work with you again a day in my life."

Still, I'm proud of the legacy Blackstreet has as one of the most influential R&B vocal groups of the 1990s alongside Guy, the two groups bookending the decade. And look at all the ways our music rippled forward: Blackstreet's "Don't Leave Me" was sampled by 2Pac on his 1996 hit "I Ain't Mad at Cha" off the ten-million-selling *All Eyez on Me*, and "No Diggity" was sampled that same year on "Toss It Up" off the *Makaveli* album. Jay-Z featured Blackstreet on his 1996 hit "The City Is Mine" off his multiplatinum debut *Reasonable Doubt*, and in the mid-2000s, Mannie Fresh would sample that hit on the Lil Wayne track "Bring it Back." Lido sampled "Don't Leave Me" on "Crazy" in 2016, and Don Toliver sampled "I Can't Get You Out of My Mind" on his 2023 hit "Bus Stop," featuring Brent Faiyaz. "Before I Let You Go" was sampled multiple times: by Freddie Gibbs in 2012, on "Money, Clothes, Hoes"; by Eric Bellinger in 2014, on "Kiss Goodnight"; and by Brian Lenair in 2018, on "Before I Let You Go." Allstar JR sampled "Joy" for his 2018 single "Million Dolla Thoughts," and "Deep" was sampled by 9th Wonder on their 2022 hit "Abyss Jam!!!"

Guy has enjoyed an even greater ripple effect in how our music has been sampled over the past thirty years, with just a few highlights including "Piece of My Love" becoming part of the 2015 hit "Play No Games" by Big Sean with Chris Brown and Ty Dolla $ign; "Run tha Streetz" by 2Pac on *All Eyez on Me*; "Money Maker," by 2Chainz featuring Lil Wayne in 2020; "Crybaby" by Mariah Carey and Snoop Dogg in 2000; "Redemption" by Jay Rock/SZA in 2018; "1999" by Big K.R.I.T. / Lloyd in 2017; "Baby Mama Blues" by Z-Ro in 2016; and "Now or Never" by Yung Fume in 2020.

Guy's "Goodbye Love" was sampled on a near constant basis,

beginning with Mary J. Blige on "Don't Go" in 1994 all the way through Nas using it on "Bye Baby" in 2012, and Siddiq on "Avante Garden with Trey" in 2019. "Let's Chill" has proven equally influential: Usher and Loon sampled it in their 2002 hit "I Need a Girl (Pt 1)"; they were followed by Don Trip and Jeremih on 2012's "Still Got Love 4 Ya," Money Mafia on 2015's "The Plug," and Chris Brown on 2022's "WE (Warm Embrace)."

But I'm especially proud of how prolifically "Teddy's Jam" has been sampled throughout multiple eras of R&B and hip-hop, from "Jam Session" by the Notorious B.I.G. and Heavy D in 1994, to Rashad's "Jam (That's My Shit)" in 2012, and SBN3's "Guy Guy." "Groove Me" was sampled by Public Enemy on 2007's "Frankenstar," and was sampled on two separate 2023 singles: "Things I Like" by Tech N9ne and "Toxic Ish" by 2rare.

As a composer and producer, it makes me beam with pride that so many generations of future stars and hitmakers have used my music as a foundation to help launch their own careers, keeping my melodies, beats, and hooks alive in the headphones, earbuds, and club and car speakers of kids growing up over the past twenty-five years and counting. I guess if people didn't want to keep hearing New Jack Swing, today's stars wouldn't sample my music in theirs, so I feel truly blessed that from Guy to Blackstreet, Bobby Brown to Michael Jackson and beyond, my sound has hung around.

CHAPTER SIXTEEN

Growing Up Riley

"In July, Riley shared a birthday tribute
to his son Mykal on Instagram."
—*PEOPLE*, 2022

When Blackstreet hit the road in 1996 in support of *Another Level*, with "No Diggity" blowing up all over radio and MTV, we were instantly catapulted to a headlining arena act. While the other guys in the band were still new to the phenomenon of being recognized by screaming fans and partying with female fans after the shows, I had gone through all that years earlier with Guy, and so when I was out on the road, for the most part I traveled on a studio bus and was pretty much always in the studio when I wasn't on stage. I didn't need to do much hanging out or messing around with girls after the shows because my life was already set by then: I was married to Donna at that point, and I was still taking care of my family at home.

I'm the proud father of nine children—four daughters, five sons altogether. When we were touring to support *Another Level*, I'd been together for sixteen years with Donna Deguzman, the mother of four of my children: my oldest daughters Deja, Taja, and Bobbie, and my son Little Teddy. I hated being away from my family in Virginia Beach, and even when I was gone on the road earning a living, I was always there for my children to make sure they had everything they wanted.

My children all went to the best private schools, and it makes me proud that they have all grown up enjoying the kind of comfortable, suburban lifestyle that I never had as a kid, even though my mother worked her heart out to give me and my siblings the best life she could. My driving motivation as a musician and producer has always been to make and maintain a better life for my family.

Growing up, my children knew I was famous from seeing me in videos on MTV, but I sheltered them from the press when they were young. More recently, though, it's been a strange transition into the digital age of social media, along with all the gossip blogs online and digital tabloids like *TMZ*, because it's been hard for me to watch my grown children having their professional and personal lives play out online now that they're in the industry themselves. It's an important reason why I chose to raise them in Virginia Beach, so that they had a "normal" childhood away from all that drama in LA or New York.

I seem to have passed on my musical DNA to my daughters. Deja, Taja, and Bobbie are all singers in a group titled R I L E Y, while my youngest daughter, Nia, has followed her father into the music business as a dancer, working with A-list acts like Shakira, Trey Songz, and Common. Nia also starred for two seasons on the VH1 reality series *Love & Hip Hop: Hollywood*, in 2015.

While my daughters have tended toward the arts, all my sons are athletes. My sixteen-year-old and thirteen-year-old both play ball, and they're both MVPs. The sixteen-year-old is ready to go into the NBA! That's how good he is, and I'm proud to say that when my thirteen-year-old was in seventh grade, he was picked to play—and start—with the eighth graders.

Their success on the court puts a big smile on my face because while I never really played basketball, and so can't teach them the game's fundamentals, I can support them the same way my family and community did when I was young and first displayed a talent for music. My father pushed me. Even though most of them didn't know how to play instruments, my family still pushed me to play and stay involved. My mom and "uncles" were a support base, and I try to do the same and support whatever my children's passions are.

For me, the most enjoyable thing about fatherhood is being able to see yourself in your kids, and to see someone you raised grow up right. That's a good feeling. The challenges have come in doing the things you have to do as a father to provide and protect them, and I applaud their mother for doing such a great job with a lot of the day-to-day parenting while I was out on the road and in the studio. I was always hustling hard to make sure that, financially, all my children would be able to have the best shot at pursuing their own dreams, which thankfully they're all doing today.

We made sure they stayed in school and went to college, and at one point, I even went broke providing for my kids and protecting them, but it was worth whatever the cost to me to make sure they had all the opportunities. I pride myself on doing for my children what I never got to do for myself when I was their age, and for loving them more than I loved myself. It hasn't fully sunk in yet that I'm a grandfather now because I still feel young and vibrant. It's almost like I don't believe I really have a granddaughter, Kameron; it's more like she's another daughter. She actually calls me Daddy.

♦ ♦ ♦ ♦ ♦

When you grow up in the music business and then join the game yourself, it can cause drama even within the most loving families. A perfect example of that intrusion—if I can jump ahead for a moment to the 2010s—would be *Love & Hip Hop*, and I'd now like to address that embarrassing public episode for my daughter for the first time in my own words.

To begin with, people have to know that there are many bad things that can happen to you in the entertainment business, and as much Gene Griffin robbed me financially, at the same time, when I was coming up, he kept me in the studio and away from all of that. I thank him for it, because otherwise I would have been sucked into the hedonistic and dark end of stardom, like the after-parties where you're constantly around drugs or other dangers. Thankfully, because my music was so in demand, the only time you saw me on TV, other than an interview with MTV, was when I was performing live or in a music video. And fortunately, in those days, that was all the media exposure you really needed.

But things had changed dramatically by the time my children were coming of age in the 2000s, with so much of the entertainment industry now driven by reality TV shows. I never wanted to be on a reality show. For years I'd been asked to do one, but other that being a judge on music competition shows like *The Voice* or *American Idol*, I had no interest in it. But it was an opportunity for my daughter Nia and her boyfriend Soulja Boy when they were approached to appear as cast members on *Love & Hip Hop: Atlanta*.

Nia asked my opinion about whether it was a good idea or not. It was an opportunity I don't blame her for taking, and I encouraged her to do it. I told her, "You'll make some money and start to make a name for yourself," but I didn't know it was going to be such a disaster. If I'd known, I wouldn't have appeared on the show. The only reason I got sucked into being part of the drama that unfolded on screen between my daughter and Soulja was because of how he mistreated her. He even suggested I wasn't her real father, but when you raise someone from the age of five into her twenties, adopt and give her your last name, you are the father. Her mother is one of my best friends and I was a true father to Nia. I'm a father who values all my daughters and protects them at all costs, even, in some cases, at the expense of my reputation in the media. Fans might remember me appearing on the *Breakfast Club* radio show to ask Soulja Boy for an apology, as a man. I eventually confronted him directly about it all, and he apologized. That's really all I prefer to say about it publicly.

I hated my family name being brought into all that drama. As much as some people like to hear their name caught up in some invented celebrity beef, I never have. When *TMZ* first broke the story, I had a sinking feeling in my stomach because I didn't want the Riley name and brand to be lowered to that level of salaciousness. I had a publicist at the time, Monica Anders, who has always been like a big sister to me and helped me navigate that media madness, and after I did the *Breakfast Club* interview in the heat of the moment, she called and advised me to "never do that again."

Monica helped me understand that my time isn't free. In the past, you had to give your time to journalists, whether it was MTV or *Spin* or *Rolling Stone* or *Vibe*—that was part of the deal. It was how you got coverage. But in the 2020s era of YouTube-and-podcast-driven interviews, the dynamic has changed, and Monica made me realize I needed to better value my time. So when Vlad TV approached me to do an interview that, to date, has millions of views and counting on YouTube, I monetized my time correctly and was able to tell my story without the tabloid press trying to twist anything I said into some obscene version. I've learned the hard way that the media will run wild with anything you say if they want to make a story out of it.

They might twist the truth into a clickbait-y headline or take a quote out of context to fit a narrative. It's frustrating to see, and it is something I try to stay as far away as possible from these days. It's part of what inspired me to write this book: to finally lay the truth out for anyone who is curious about my life, directly from me, with no filter or editor or journalist trying to bend my words to fit some headline.

♦ ♦ ♦ ♦ ♦

There are times in my life that the pressures of being in the public eye have just been so draining, especially with as huge as Blackstreet got in the '90s. We were selling out arenas all over the world, winning Grammys, dominating radio, and by the late 1990s, I was exhausted. Once our world tour wrapped in 1997 as a blockbuster success, I took a hiatus. The record business was changing drastically with the advent of Napster and downloading, and I felt alienated from it. The music business is a game, and I felt like I no longer wanted to deal with all the people who basically hated on me for being so successful. Seriously, haters are out there, and their MO at the time was: "Teddy Riley's making all these records, doing all these hits, so we've got to figure out a way to move him out of the way." I kept my relationships with people like Jimmy Iovine, who has always been there for me, but others were not. Fortunately, I was doing well enough financially to buy time and take care of myself for the next few years, and I moved to California around 2000.

I loved the anonymity of LA, especially after living for years as the biggest star in a city as small as Virginia Beach, where I was regularly recognized whenever I was out in public, eating at restaurants, or even at the grocery store. After Blackstreet blew up with "No Diggity," it got even more intense, but in LA, I could go out and be myself. I could shop and be regular with my family. That said, it never bothered me when a fan stopped me in public and asked for a picture or an autograph because that's what we sign up for as stars, and it's important to honor fans and to not hide behind that aura of celebrity. Treating fans with the respect and generosity they deserve ensures that they will continue to support you by coming out to see your concerts and buying your records. People don't think about that: When you turn fans off by acting like there's an invisible line between you and them, they're also turned off from buying your records. I was never that way, so people never said about me, "He's a conceited bastard. He's so *Hollywood*."

It comes with the territory: All fans want to do is interact with you, even for a moment, and while those moments may seem to blur together for the celebrity who signs and takes a million autographs and photos, each one lasts forever for the fans. That was their moment with you, and it's something I've said to younger entertainers for years when they've asked me for advice: Never ignore your fans. That's especially true today in the age of cell phone cameras and social media, where we have more of a chance to connect directly with our supporters.

Even back before email, I always made sure to read and answer all of my fan mail. I have signed and sent out thousands of requested/signed fan pics and autographed photos over the years. Some of my fans' letters have even moved me so much that they became the inspiration for hits I wrote, like Guy's "Let's Chill" and Blackstreet's "Don't Leave Me" and "Before I Let Go." So no matter the medium, my underlying philosophy is the same: Show your fans the same love they're showing you.

Now, there are some that go ballistic, and there are many, many, many who will go crazy just being in the same room with you. Over the years, I've seen girls faint, cry, all of that. Even then, I still try to treat everyone with the same respect, because at the end of the day, the reason they're so excited is because of the way my music made them feel.

Still, within the industry, the early 2000s were definitely a time of transition. I remember reading a book, *Who Moved My Cheese?* by Spencer Johnson, which deals with change and how the attitude we bring to it can impact the outcome. I said to myself, "You know what? Music is changing, and I don't want to change my music, but I have to change *with* the music," as I'd done after the 1980s with Michael Jackson on *Dangerous* and with Blackstreet then dominating another decade.

By then, Guy fans were clamoring for a new album because we'd been apart for a decade. I managed to pull together the Hall brothers, put our differences aside, and reenter the studio to record our third and final album, *Guy III*. That said, the studio has always been my favorite place to be with Aaron Hall, aside from the stage. It's where we spend our best time and always did what we do best together: making music. We'd continue touring our catalog together through the 2000s to fans all over the world. But it was clear to me that was going to be the end of recording music with Guy, and we never made another new album after that.

◆ ◆ ◆ ◆ ◆

Sadly, as well as things were going on the road and in the studio, back home in Virginia Beach, my world was rocked by a financial scandal after I fell victim to a swindler named Troy Titus in the early 2000s. He is a monster and con man—currently doing decades in prison—who took me for several million dollars in a real estate fraud that eventually earned him his very own episode of the CNBC television show *American Greed*. This guy basically took everything from me: I lost my home, my studio, my cars, pretty much all I owned, and I had to file for bankruptcy.

As embarrassing as that was, I was desperate because of the position he had put me in, and bankruptcy was the only way for me to get me out from under the load of debt Troy had accrued in my name and to start over. He had run a multimillion-dollar Ponzi scheme on me and other victims in the Virginia Beach area, ultimately taking us for almost $20 million in total. He wound up being convicted in federal court on thirty-three felony counts of fraud and is now doing thirty years in prison. But when I first met him, he seemed like a legitimate financial guru, promising he could help me out of the difficult situation I found myself in at the time. Apparently, he fooled a lot of his victims with the same charm.

When you're in a business like I'm in, that's the type of crap you have to look out for, and bankruptcy aside, recovering from the financial devastation of the Troy Titus swindle required prayer, resilience, and a lot of musical inspiration as I played my way out of the hole for the second time in my life. Just as I'd done following the catastrophe with Gene Griffin, in putting Troy Titus in my rearview mirror, I chose to focus on reinventing my New Jack Swing sound for the new millennium and introducing it to a new generation.

I worked hard during this period to make sure I protected my kids from the scandal and bankruptcy. I didn't let them know what I was going through and made sure it wasn't out there as news, so that they didn't have to walk to school and hear some little kid say, "Your dad . . ." in any negative context. They never had kids making fun of their father, which was important to me.

Fortunately, I found that a generation of musicians who had grown up listening to my records and watching me on MTV were now coming into stardom in their own right, and many eagerly sought me out in the studio, which got me out of debt and gave me and my family a fresh start heading into the 2000s. But what a crazy ride it was getting there.

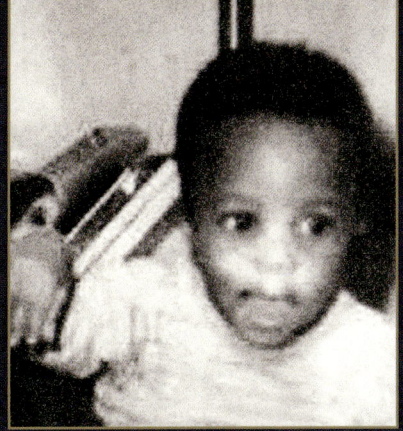

LEFT

As a toddler, circa 1968.

BELOW

My biological father,
Roger Clement, 1970.

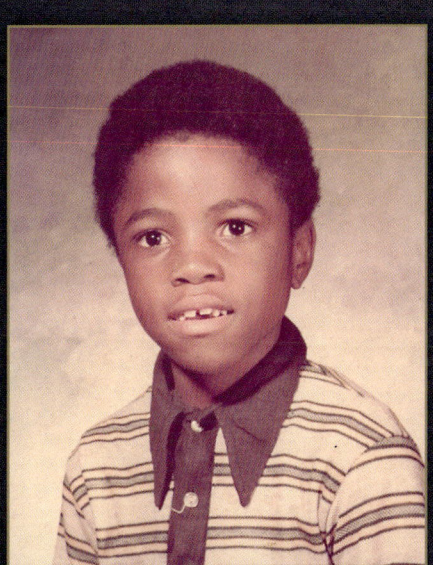

ABOVE

Me, age eight, in a
mid–1970s school photo.

RIGHT

My sister, Joyce, and
cousin Raymond with our
great-grandmother
down south, 1975.

TOP LEFT

With my younger brother, Markell, and my mom, Mildred, in Harlem, 1977.

CENTER LEFT

Front, from left to right: Aunt Edith, me at age fifteen, Aunt Elizabeth Washington, and my grandmother Lucile Washington. Back, from left to right: Uncle Butchie and Aunt Marlene, cousin Chris, cousin Lucy, and my mother, Mildred.

BELOW

Performing as a kid at a Kids at Work rehearsal. From right to left: I'm on organ, Larry Gatling is on drums, Timmy Gatling is on bass, Clurel Henderson is in white, and Tawona T is on the far left.

TOP LEFT

In the projects in the 1980s. I was excited about my new The Winans "It's Time" license plate frames.

CENTER LEFT

In front of Palladium in 1986; Guy would eventually play our first show there.

ABOVE RIGHT

With Keith Sweat in 1988.

RIGHT

In the studio, late 1980s.

LEFT
With my former manager, Gene Griffin, and Eddie Murphy, circa 1989.

ABOVE, LEFT & RIGHT
In the studio, circa 1990.

RIGHT
Me and producer Frank Kemp, 1990. We worked on James Ingram's music together.

LEFT
*My studio
in Virginia
Beach, 1991.*

RIGHT
Guy in 1991.

BELOW LEFT
Tom Joyner and Guy.

BELOW RIGHT
*Posing with my Guy
bandmates and fans at
a concert, circa 1991.*

LEFT
*In the studio in the early
1990s working on a
Blackstreet album.*

RIGHT
*With Michael Jackson at
Larrabee Studios, Los Angeles,
working on* Dangerous, *1991.*

BELOW
*With Michael, standing
next to the Commodore
Sampler that I programmed
"Remember the Time" on.*

TOP LEFT

In the studio with Heavy D & the Boyz, circa 1992. Heavy D is second from the left.

TOP RIGHT

At the Billboard Music Awards, 1993, with the group H-Town.

CENTER RIGHT

Celebrating my twenty-eighth birthday in Miami, 1995.

BOTTOM RIGHT

With (from left) Heavy D, Montell Jordan, and Jermaine Dupri in Florida, 1995.

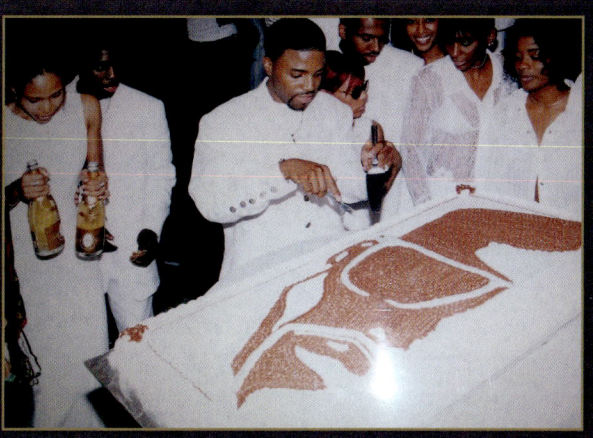

TOP LEFT

*At the record deal signing
party for the vocal group
5th Avenue, circa 1996.*

CENTER LEFT

*With Chauncey Black, Jermaine
Dupri, and Queen Pen, 1996.*

BELOW

*Blackstreet, 112, Lil G from Silk,
and actress Michelle Thomas at the
1997 Soul Train Music Awards.*

With Michael Jackson and Sisqó, circa 2000.

With my daughter Taja and friend, late 1990s.

From left to right: security team of Big Wayne (RIP), me, sensei Tony Watts, and Big Dave (RIP).

With legendary producer Quincy Jones, circa 2008.

With Lady Gaga in the Record Plant in Los Angeles, 2009.

With actor Jamie Foxx in 2010.

With Pharrell Williams, whom I found in 1991.

With Stevie Wonder at NAAM, 2012.

TOP LEFT

With my mother, Mildred; granddaughter, Kamryn; and sons Samar and Teddy Jr. after delivering the 2015 commencement speech at Georgia Piedmont Technical College.

TOP RIGHT

With my godfather Benjamin Wright.

LEFT

With coauthor Jake Brown in October 2015 at the Fox Theatre in Atlanta.

RIGHT

With my sister, Joyce, and mom, circa 2015.

TOP RIGHT

With Ludacris at his annual event, LudaDay Weekend, circa 2015.

CENTER RIGHT

With boxing legend Floyd Mayweather and singer Tank at a Manny Pacquiao fight, Las Vegas, Nevada, May 2, 2015.

BELOW

With J-Styles and Ice Cube in 2014.

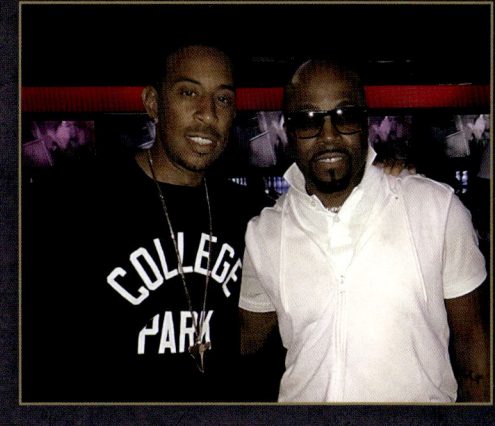

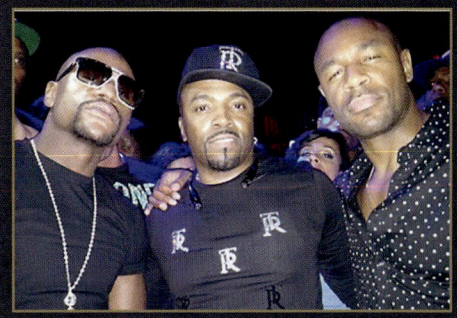

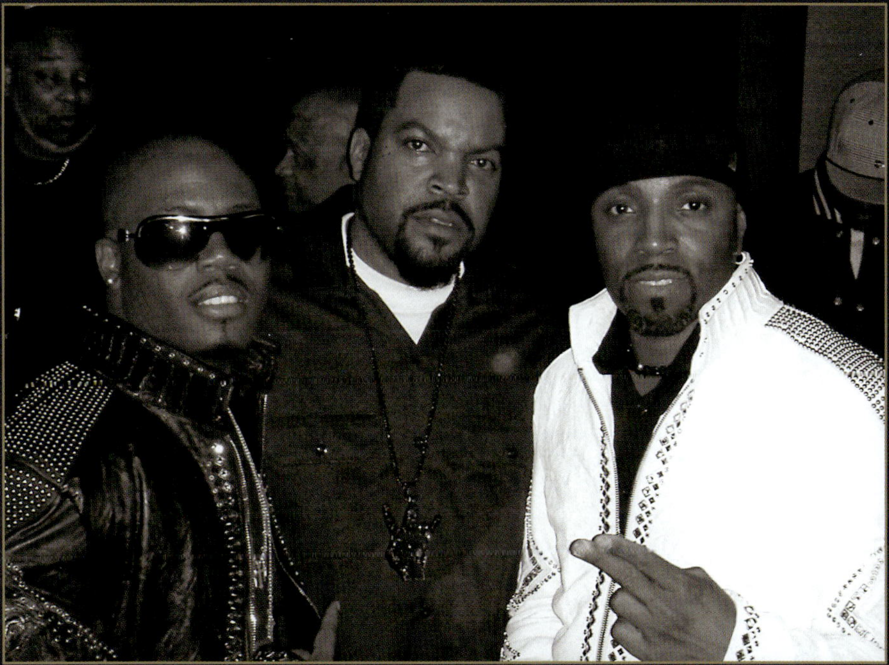

LEFT

Working at the studio on the Ego Trippin' *album with DJ Quik and hip-hop duo Tha Dogg Pound's Kurupt and Snoop Dogg.*

BELOW

With Public Enemy's Flavor Flav and producer/DJ Eric B. in 2019.

ABOVE

With Rapper Biz Markie.

RIGHT

With Don King, the iconic boxing promoter, in Miami, Florida, in 2017.

ABOVE

With my daughters (from left to right) Bobbie, Deja, Nia, and Taja in 2019, celebrating getting my star on the Hollywood Walk of Fame.

LEFT

During a prison visit in the 2010s with my spiritual brother Lou Hobbs, a few years before he was pardoned.

RIGHT

My cousin Lucy, sister Nece, adopted son Dante, niece Crystal, mother, and daughters Bobbie and Taja with friends at graduation ceremony in 1999.

TOP LEFT
With Mike Tyson and T.K. Kirkland, January 2020.

TOP RIGHT
With my brother at the Apollo Theatre, Harlem, NY, 2019.

LEFT
With Kenny "Babyface" Edmonds, circa 2024.

BELOW
Meeting Rev. Al Sharpton at the Essence Awards, 2019.

CHAPTER SEVENTEEN

The 2000s

"It's because of Riley's pugilistic spirit that he remains a viable force in the music industry over 25 years after he first broke in the biz. It's why he is equally in-demand by hip-hop royalty (Snoop Dogg) as he is by modern day, censor-igniting pop icons."

—VIBE

The new millennium kept me as busy and blessed as ever as I bounced back from the brink of financial ruin for the second time in my career, courtesy of superstars like Mariah Carey (on "Crybaby" off her *Rainbow* LP) and Jodeci's K-Ci and JoJo (on "Wanna Do You Right" from their *X* album) and the new generation of stars like Queen Pen, with "I Got Cha" from her *Conversations with Queen* LP, and Sisqó's "Can I Live" from his *Return of Dragon*.

I also worked with Spice Girl Melanie B on tracks like "ABC 123," "I Believe," and "Pack Your S**t" for her debut solo album,

Hot. One of my favorite calls came when NSYNC sought me out to work on their monster 13-million seller *No Strings Attached.* The band and I produced a new version of my Johnny Kemp classic "Just Got Paid," a tribute of sorts to their own roots growing up on my New Jack sound.

The reverberations of my music kept the phone ringing off the hook, including a call I was blessed and so happy to answer—it was Michael Jackson on the other end of the line inviting me to work on his *Invincible* album, which was released in 2001. I felt like a proud papa when he explained that he and my protégé Rodney Jerkins were already hard at work on the record. What put the biggest smile on my face was when he told me how well they were jelling in the studio. It was a bit of a vision come true, one I'd had back when I was working with Michael on *Dangerous* and had first put Rodney's name in his ear, mentioning him as someone I predicted Michael would be working with in the future.

When I was in the studio working with Michael on *Invincible*, there was some friendly creative competition at play, because Michael and the other people involved with the project were basically challenging me against Rodney. At that point in time, I felt like Rodney did well with the record, and all I could do was add to that magic, so that's what I did. But Michael would play the songs Rodney had produced and ask, "Well, what would you do to this?"

I found out from Rodney that Michael would do the same thing with him: play the songs I'd produced and ask, "What would you do to this?" I took some of Rodney's suggestions, and he did the same. It was a strategy Michael used to great effect, challenging us all to bring our best to the console. We worked together on songs like "Heaven Can Wait," "2000 Watts," "Don't Walk Away," and "Whatever Happens," which, as a bonus, marked my first time working with Carlos Santana, who played a lead guitar solo on the track.

In 2003, I managed to pull off another Blackstreet album, *Level II*, with Chauncey Hannibal and the other original members of the group. It would sadly prove to be our final studio collaboration. One of the greatest drawbacks of longevity, which I've seen plague groups like a cancer, is ego. It's the double-edged sword of success in the record business.

I'd been through it with Guy a decade before, and after everything I'd been through with Troy Titus only a few years earlier, I didn't have the spiritual energy for any more stress like that in my world. I was lucky that I could still make a nice living staying in the studio and touring as a solo act, so I decided to focus for the next few years on making records with what I'm proud to say proved to be a really hip, contemporary list of collaborators.

One highlight was working with Britney Spears on a smash hit update to "My Prerogative" for her first greatest hits album, in 2004. It became a huge hit on MTV and a Top 5 hit on the British

Pop Charts, peaking at number three. Britney had the press and paparazzi after her like I'd only seen them go after Bobby Brown and Michael Jackson before, and I was proud she chose that song to be her answer, her anthem of defiance, which introduced me to a whole new nation of teenage music fans.

I found myself in the studio soon thereafter working with a true New York hip-hop legend, LL Cool J, on "I'm About to Get Her" from his 2004 album, *The DEFinition*, which gave me another Top 5 album on the Billboard Top 200 Album Chart. It took me back to my vintage days making rap tracks in the projects, feeling the heat of the street in the beat. Knowing we could still deliver that kind of hard edge to the track was an almost indescribable feeling. LL loves when his producers bring the fire in the studio, and I was more than happy to accommodate him.

For all the time I was spending with new artists in the studio, I kept touring throughout the 2000s, playing to the loyal fans who had stuck with me from the beginning. It was such a blessing to hear their cheers and listen to them singing along every night to a catalog that had truly been the soundtrack of their lives, as clichéd as that sounds. Some nights, it was just as powerful looking out into a crowd and seeing lifelong fans bringing their *kids* along to the shows, and then seeing those kids singing the same songs line for line with their parents.

One of the most amazing concerts we put on was seen not only by the local fans who sold out the Hammerstein Ballroom in my hometown, but also by the millions watching around the world on cable that night. This was the night of the VH1 Hip Hop Honors, September 25, 2007. I had by then become known for my "Teddy Riley and Friends"–style revue where I'd often feature on the bill different collaborators of all genres, from hip-hop to R&B to pop and beyond, to give the audience the most bang for their buck. One of the mothers of all such reunion concerts happened that night. The crowd went wild for it, and so did the press, because we were all over the news the next day.

The night wound up on a high note when I was inducted into the Songwriters Hall of Fame, with Doug E. Fresh and Keith Sweat presenting me my award. It felt amazing to see how far New Jack Swing had traveled as a music genre, but it's also strange when you're responsible for helping bring something new into the world. It's comparable to having a child, then watching them first walk, talk, and sing (in the case of many of my children). I shake my head sometimes because I was so young myself when my musical genre was first blowing up on the streets and club dance floors and then radio and video.

That love of New Jack Swing remained as alive around the world as it was here in the States, because right after that VH1 show, I hopped on the private jet with my band that our promoter had been kind enough to charter and flew to Japan to play a series of sold-out arena shows. We played back-to-back nights in Osaka that fall, then topped 2007 off by playing a New Year's Eve show in Taiwan.

◆ ◆ ◆ ◆ ◆

One sad moment during these otherwise bright days came when I got the call that my beloved Future Studios had burned down. I'd been moved out of there for years by then, so I didn't lose anything personally in the way of gear or mementos, but I had so many wonderful musical memories within those four magical walls that I'll always treasure.

I sat down recently and flipped through the fantastic discography we created there, and it stunned me. Just to name a few: SWV's *It's About Time* album, featuring the massive hit "Right Here (Human Nature Remix)"; Wreckx-n-Effect's "Rump Shaker," another massive radio and video hit; Bobby Brown's *Bobby* album with his hit duet with Whitney Houston, "Something in Common"; MC Lyte's *Ain't No Other* LP; Patti LaBelle's *Gems* album; a very talented R&B girl group Pure Soul's eponymous debut; Foxy Brown's *Ill Na Na*; Taral Hicks's *This Time*; Usher's multiplatinum *My Way*; Queen Pen's *My Melody*; Lord Tariq & Peter Gunz's *Make It Reign*; Kelly Price's *Mirror Mirror*; Joe's *My Name Is Joe*; former Spice Girl Melanie B's solo album *Hot*; Method Man's "Party & Bulls***"; and, to top it all off, Janet Jackson's singles "I Get Lonely" and "Go Deep." We had quite a run!

♦ ♦ ♦ ♦ ♦

As 2009 came to a close, I found myself working with Robin Thicke on his new album *Sex Therapy: The Session*. Robin is a gifted artist to work with in the studio, and we wound up writing and producing the single "It's in the Mornin'" together. An important footnote to the Robin Thicke collaboration was the guest appearance on the single by Snoop Dogg, who loved what he heard when we played him the track we wanted him to rap on. Snoop and I had reconnected at the VH1 Hip Hop Honors back in 2007 when we were both sitting in the same balcony. Until it was time for us to perform, he and I were just sitting there conversing. It surprised me when he said, "Yo, come to California to work with me. Come next week." I was flattered, but that was when I was taking my hiatus from producing. I was being honored at various award shows and wasn't into making music. I was just into my kids. But after I made that appearance, Snoop called me up and insisted, "Saddle up! I need you to come out and work with me on the *Ego Trippin'* album." So first I had to talk to my kids about it, because we'd just moved to Atlanta, and they were like, "Dad, it's Snoop Dogg! *Go!*"

Working with Snoop was like working with a family member—a cousin, a brother—because we shared not only the studio time but also the spirit and chemistry. *Ego Trippin'* would mark a monumental recording moment in hip-hop history because of the all-star team of producers Snoop put together to helm the project—not just me but

Scott Storch, DJ Quik, J.R. Rotem, the Neptunes, Scoop DeVille, Raphael Saadiq, and more. As usual, I prepared music beforehand—Snoop gave me that time—and when I came out to LA, I played a bunch of records for him in the studio. Once we got into the studio for proper sessions, the atmosphere was magical. Snoop was spontaneous, but when he did his singing, he liked to do that alone; I got to be in only a couple of sessions.

I was working not only with Snoop but also the legendary West Coast rapper-producer DJ Quik. As a trio, we called ourselves the "QDT." We wanted to make a record where musicians would be like, "Wow!" and that's what we got. I would get musicians coming up to me all the time saying, "Yo, that *Ego Trippin'* record—QDT, man!" When I got that, I knew that I had accomplished something. Mind you, we were in the social network era now, too. Kids would hit me up on Twitter and say, "Man, what you did to that record, no other producer has ever done that for Snoop Dogg. You really took him to music and jamming." There's a real reward for me when I get an artist to try something, and see how it feels, in the studio. It can't hurt you. You can only gain.

Snoop actually got me an apartment at Sunset and Vine, in Hollywood, because he had one in the same building. It was a vibrant place. Ty Dolla $ign was living a few doors down from me, but the funny thing was, I was on what was considered to be the "quiet side" of the building. When I would play my music, neighbors would call to complain. Snoop's apartment was over on what they considered to be the "cool side" of the building, where everybody was making all the noise. I wanted to move over there! But I was at Snoop's so much working that it felt like I was staying there. It was a very creative vibe: I got a lot of the music done in that building and Snoop did a lot of his vocal tracking in his apartment. He used an old Telefunken vocal microphone, which made me buy that microphone to add to my collection.

When we weren't recording out of the apartment, we were working at Encore Studios, in Burbank, and ultimately went from there to another studio in Burbank to finish the album. Snoop had a bunch of rooms going on at once, and it was myself, DJ Quik, and Terrence Martin, and Tha Dogg Pound, Kurupt, and Daz Dillinger came through. At the same time, we did something with Robin Thicke, a record called "It's in the Mornin'," and it was all a great synergy.

For all the highlights the first decade of the 2000s gave me, I experienced one of my greatest lows professionally and personally on June 25, 2009, when I watched with tears in my eyes and a heavy heart on cable news as Michael Jackson was driven in an ambulance to the hospital. He died shortly thereafter, and as the world reacted, I was proud to see that prominently noted was his work helping take New Jack Swing to its peak of popularity around the world. Having a star like Michael Jackson touch your music makes it shine—it's just that simple. My music had always been street with a pop polish, but Michael and I managed to make a sound as sleek as the fashion runways and trendy dance floors while still being as street as the boom boxes that were playing our sound around Harlem just as loudly. It was a sound heard around the world thanks to Michael, from New York City to Africa and every continent and country in between, and we were both always so proud of that.

The last time I ever spoke with Michael was about three months before he passed. He wanted me to come out to LA and work with him on "This Is It." We still had details to work out when the next Michael-related call I got came from a friend of mine on the day he died. She was crying, and the first thing she could get out was, "Did you hear? Michael's dead," and I fell down on the floor. I couldn't believe it. He was so excited to go back in the studio to produce some new songs for the project, and that was always the greatest memory I had of him: being in the studio making the music and the two of us having this synergy back and forth with key decisions. The fun we had being creative, the flow that got going between us—it was like no other artist I've ever worked with before or since.

Looking back on my twenty years of knowing and working with Michael Jackson, my favorite songs of all the music we made together are definitely "In the Closet" and "Why You Wanna Trip on Me?" The second one is special because I came up with it on the spot. I remember Michael saying to me, "I want something that's gonna kill! I want something that's just gonna . . ." and before he could even finish, I was already hearing music in my head. I told him, "Michael, please leave the room for a minute."

Well, he was both surprised and intrigued when he heard that, because it was not usually something I said to him when we were working together. When he asked me why I wanted him to go away for a bit, I bravely replied, "Because you want something that's gonna kill, and the only way that I'm going to kill you is if you leave, and then when you walk back in the door, that's when I'll play the music, and if it doesn't kill you, then walk back out the door." He bought that, left me for a little while, and when he did come back in, the instant he heard the first sixty seconds of that song's beat, he said, "Oh my God!" He started dancing, then asked, "That's for me?" I said, "Of course . . ."

From there, he didn't want to leave the room again, he was so in love with the song, and that was how we usually knew we had something when we were collaborating, because from my instrumental, he started hearing melodies in his head. We had some really hot tracks that were released in 2006 on *Visionary: The Video Singles*, a box set that included a late 1990s single, "Blood on the Dance Floor." Michael and I had kept our sound spinning around the world for nearly two decades by then, and we'd often talk together about it on the phone.

We had remained close friends right up to his tragic death. It was an incredible thing, being a friend of Michael's, because a lot of people can't say that, and our friendship was more than just us doing music; it was family oriented. I was like the cousin or little brother, and I would get calls through the years where he'd say, "I need to talk to you about something. I need your ears—do you have time?" And of course, I would always make time. We would get into aspects of doing music and talking about music, and where it was going from here. I was always so honored that Michael trusted me deeply enough to share his musical visions for the future with me.

He would get so deep into the philosophy of music. There were times during our conversations when he'd rattle off an idea, and I'd take it upon myself, once we'd hung up, to go into my studio and produce a demo of his idea, then send it to him and ask, "Are you talking about something like this?" It was those kinds of conversations preceding my heading into the studio to work with him again on *Invincible* during which we developed the songs we wound up producing together, along with tracks that didn't see the light of day until 2010's posthumous *Michael* record, with which we gave the world one more hit with "Hollywood Tonight," which peaked at number one on the Billboard Dance/Club Play Songs Chart. Whenever I hear music we'd made together on the radio or a streaming service, it makes me feel a little melancholy, because though I know the music we recorded together made history, we still had plans for more to come, and that chance passed with him.

✦ ✦ ◆ ✦ ✦

I wound up with a surprise number one hit in Britain when Shout for England—made up of Dizzee Rascal and James Corden—topped the singles chart there for four weeks in 2010 with "Shout," which sampled "No Diggity." Then, Boyz II Men honored me with a call to work on the *Twenty* album, for which we made "Believe" and "Flow" together. It was amazing to hear those classic harmonies coming to life on top of my tracks.

Lady Gaga asked me to work on a single for her multiplatinum *Fame Monster* album. That was very cool because it was the first time since Michael Jackson that I'd worked with anyone who was a director and a composer, and also a visionary for all of their projects. All I had to do was come up with the music, or score, for her titles. That's what she does: She names the songs on the album beforehand. She had the title "Show Me Your Teeth" and a demo of how she would perform the song, humming it and banging on a table.

I put that demo in my sequencer and scored the music to it. With my sequencer, Cubase, you can take a voice note off a phone like the one she sent me, load it into the sequencer, and sync it up, and once I synced it up to the click track, I started flowing. Once I sent it to Gaga and her team, they said, "Okay, let's go into the studio," and it went that quick, thanks to her manager, Vincent Herbert.

It was a wild session because there was a horn section that came in to track while Lady Gaga and I were both there, plus background singers, while I produced her vocal track. Unlike most other recording sessions I produce where I'm running the show, Lady Gaga was working right alongside me throughout the session as a coproducer. She's very talented musically and as a songwriter, and she can tell you everything from the key she's singing in to notes on the production she had as we were working.

The only downside to the Lady Gaga collaboration came when we ran into a small conflict over music publishing for the song, now called "Teeth." As a loving father in a volatile industry, I've learned that one of the only sure long-term revenue streams that a songwriter can provide his family is through music publishing. Throughout my career, on different hits, I've put part of my publishing in my children's names so that they have a future revenue stream from that song's use in movies, TV, streaming, and whatever else might come along in the future. I gave my daughter Taja Riley, who was then nineteen, a co-credit on "Teeth." Sadly, not long afterward, in service of her own ambition, Taja would represent herself as an actual songwriter on that song, which she was in no way, shape, or form. She then went about literally selling the publishing out from under me.

Surreally, my daughter and I wound up in court over the whole thing. Ultimately the case was resolved legally and I forgave my daughter for it. I still love her to death, but I had to learn to take the high road of forgiveness because when someone in your family does something to you, the only thing you can do is challenge it and forgive them. Sadly, it's a more common story in the music business than you'd believe.

CHAPTER EIGHTEEN

K-Pop

"Rap's minimalist palette still rules much of American pop. But some writers with bridges to spare have found an unexpected—though not unwelcome—refuge in South Korea, where K-Pop artists still treasure the songcraft that persisted in R&B's mainstream until the early 2000s . . . In a musical marketplace with those reference points, it makes sense that American R&B mavens would be in demand. Teddy Riley, the American singer-songwriter-producer famous for his work with acts like Keith Sweat, Guy and Blackstreet, was one of the first to make the trip to South Korea, (first) flying out in 2009 and establishing a sideline as a New Jack Swing savant for Girls' Generation and Jay Park."

—ROLLING STONE

To push forward through my grief, I naturally took refuge in the studio and the music therapy of making new hits in Michael Jackson's honor. I kicked off the 2010s with another trip overseas, this time not to perform live but instead to work on the cutting edge of a new sound just beginning to bubble up on the charts—K-Pop. I'd decided to take my sound international, leading me to take up creative residence in Japan, where I began working with a whole new generation of pop stars who were emerging from the booming K-Pop scene across Asia.

It was a surreal position I found myself in: Here I was, once again, on the ground floor of this newly born genre, helping guide its first era of stars. It began with Girls' Generation on what would become their smash single "The Boys" for their debut album. I was invigorated making new music, and as soon as that first single hit radio, it spread like wildfire and the calls kept coming in. I next worked with another rising act, the boy band SHINee, on the hits "Beautiful," "SHINe," and "Dangerous." I also wrote and produced "All Night" and "MILK" for f(x)'s studio album *Red Light* and the single "What is Love" for EXO.

To tell the truth, I have always gotten a bigger kick out of working with new artists than established ones. Why is that? Because when

I created New Jack Swing, it was made by new artists. Bobby Brown was considered new when he did New Jack Swing, and the established artists who did it revived themselves almost as if they were new artists. Listen to Janet Jackson's *Rhythm Nation* album. That's New Jack Swing, nobody can doubt that—Janet's producers Jimmy Jam and Terry Lewis had to jump on the bandwagon—and I embraced that as a compliment. I embraced it because the world knows I created New Jack Swing, and I did what I did so that we could have our own generation of music, not our elders' generation, and our own history. The exciting thing now was that not only was the K-Pop sound blowing up in the Pacific Rim, but it would soon enough take America by storm.

I have always loved the constant "go, go, go" pace of the music industry. It's what drives me and keeps me working, knowing that I'm still received and appreciated, and knowing that the music is still appreciated. If I were to leave this earth tomorrow, it would be knowing I have true fans that love the music that I brought to this earth and that I've been a part of, so to have channeled that passion and endless musical energy into helping create another new sound was quite a rush. That it was patterned and built on a sound I'd created over twenty years earlier was even more incredible to me, because it meant that my music not only held up and had stood the tests of time but also served as a foundation for further innovation.

Thanks to the advent of recording virtually, I was still producing new acts in America while living in Japan. We were now living in the Jetsons' era of record production. One notable act I produced that way was a promising new Atlanta-based group known as Final Draft that included amazing vocalists in Fashun, Voice, D-Nyce, Lucky, and Divine. One of the highlights we created together in the studio was a track called "Do It," which featured guest appearances from Yung Joc and J-Bar of SODMG.

♦ ♦ ◆ ♦ ♦

While I enjoyed my residency working in Japan during the height of the K-Pop boom, I returned to living in the States by 2012, settling with my family in Atlanta. The city was a hotbed for new talent coming out of the South, and I began working with the hottest new artists making noise on the streets, not only Final Draft but also acts like Melinda Santiago, Rudy Currence, Akua Bishop, Jason Ikeem Rodgers, The Anointed Pace Sisters, and The Bad Rabbits. I also went into the studio with some vets of the ATL including Lloyd, Pleasure P, and Jacob Latimore.

In August of 2012, I was honored to be presented by ASCAP with Atlanta's prestigious ICON Award at the ATL Live on the Park Festival, where Blackstreet headlined and were supported by even more gifted Atlanta artists on the rise, including Marques Anthony, Amber Bullock, Mishon, and Brittnee Camelle. The day was topped off when Mayor Kasim Reed and City Council President Ceasar Mitchell jointly presented me with a proclamation from the City of Atlanta. It was all quite humbling.

Thankfully, especially given the competition out there, I was blessed that the stars kept lining up to work with me, including Nas, who, when asked who was at the top of his wish list of producers to work with on new material, told New York's hottest hip-hop radio station, Hot 97, "I would love to do something with Teddy Riley!" Prince's former protégé Tevin Campbell rang me up to help work on his first comeback album in nearly fifteen years, and through my label Teddy Riley Music Group (TRMG), I signed Bollywood star Rishi Rich, and we had a roll-out in London.

All the while, I kept touring with Blackstreet featuring the great Dave Hollister, and whether we were playing the Hard Rock Café in Vegas or headlining the Essence Festival in Atlanta, we always had sold-out crowds on their feet singing along for the whole show, which is always my favorite reaction as I try to make every show I do the best one of my career.

My children, all of whom have grown up "at my feet," so to speak, in the record industry, were starting to come of age by then, with my eldest three daughters being the first to take the dive. I was so proud when Bobbie, Taja, and Deja got in the family business and formed a group together, releasing their first single, "ATM," in 2011. It was fun to appear as a guest star with my daughter Deja on the hit VH1 reality show *Growing Up Hip Hop*.

A father's greatest fears and hopes revolve around what his children will do with their dreams and lives, and while you can't pick who they love, it was fun for me to watch that show and see Deja living her life, in the business and out. She has such a good head on her shoulders. Today, I have a better balance between being able to focus on my family and kids while still making music, and personally, in the past few years, have tried to focus on my own happiness now that my oldest children are out in the world doing their own thing. I've always felt in the end that we're all masters of our own momentum, and though God has always guided my journey, it's been through my sheer blood, sweat, tears, and hard work that I've been able to keep the Teddy Riley music machine in motion for so many decades now.

I'm just giving you a real look behind the scenes of what it takes to operate on a "superstar" level. As the boss, I have a band to run and keep paid; a road crew to make sure everything gets from gig to gig without breaking down on the side of the highway hauling a sixteen-wheeler with all our gear; promoters to deal with once I get to those cities; along with the local press, who I always welcome, but who add yet another layer of personalities to manage as I give interviews to the local papers. Then I have to make time before and after shows to visit with the many dear friends I've made across the country through all my years touring. On top of that, there are typically VIP fan meet-and-greets before we even get on stage. Luckily, that's where I'm happiest, on stage, where I feel like all that hard work and grind touring from one city to the next is worth it, when I hear the cheer of the crowd, see the smiles on their faces singing along.

It has always made me very proud to know we have and continue to make that connection with audiences. We put 1,000 percent into every show, no phoning it in. I go into another zone and by the time the crowd is cheering for more even after the encore, we walk off stage knowing we've left it all out there. Think about this too: These days, you don't just have the eyes and ears of the immediate audience you're performing for, because lighters have been replaced with smartphones that record and rebroadcast your performance on YouTube the same night and forever after for anyone and everyone to see. That gives performers an extra pressure to give their all every night, realizing just how many eyes are watching them in the moment and well into the future.

◆ ◆ ◆ ◆ ◆

My second job kicks in after the show is over and I return to my bus or hotel room, where I always have studios set up so I can get whatever new music that is playing in my head out and onto a track. When I'm not performing or working on my own music, I'm often making remixes for artists all over the world, which means I stay busier at times than I'd like to.

Music has always been my drug, and I'm so grateful I've steered clear my entire life of drugs of any kind. I have never been much of a drinker, either, because music always gave me my high. But taking care of myself has always been a challenge with so many others to put first, whether fans or family, and so while I'll always continue to take care of my loved ones, these days, I'm doing a better job of trying to take care of myself.

I was lucky to have planted my seeds early and achieved everything I wanted to musically. I'm lucky that I'm still doing it today. I'm lucky that people continue to enjoy everything that's musical about me and keep saying, "Please release another one." That's thanks to me being innovative and trying things that people have never heard before. But the creative, musical side is only part of it: My physical, mental, and emotional health are key to my longevity too. That was an important realization for me. It's important to keep it all in balance. For a happy life, you have to harmonize. That's something I've always tried to impart to the producers that have come up under my wing over the past four decades, because I've seen so many come and go who didn't.

In my heart, I've always gotten the greatest joy from bringing it to others, both in my music and in how I try to give back to the community. That's a tradition that was bred into me growing up in Harlem, whether I watched the local gangsters giving out turkeys at Thanksgiving and presents to the kids at Christmas or saw the local churches or Harlem Globetrotters team, or even the Guardian Angels, doing the same. Everybody chipped in and did their part. As I saw firsthand growing up in the projects, many of those families wouldn't have had holiday meals or presents without these benefactors, and it's a tradition I'm proud to continue each year.

My music continued making enough noise heading toward the 2020s that more legacy organizations were starting to acknowledge me, as the National Museum of African American Music did in

2022 when I was honored alongside Kirk Franklin, Patti LaBelle, and David Porter at the museum's Legends Luncheon. This was part of the "My Music Matters" campaign celebrating "black artists who have made a significant impact on American musical culture." Equally humbling was the night in 2018 when Bruno Mars acknowledged me on stage in his acceptance speech when his *24K Magic* won the biggest Grammy Award of the night for Album of the Year, where he kindly told the crowd, "I'd like to dedicate this award to Teddy Riley, Babyface, and Jimmy Jam and Terry Lewis. They're my heroes. They are my teachers; they laid the foundation where this album wouldn't exist if it wasn't for these guys."

Just seeing that on TV was something. I'd never met Bruno Mars, but I appreciated his tribute. It felt even more incredible when my kids called me, because my shine is their shine. It also made Dad look super cool to all their friends, who are growing up on Bruno Mars now! So I'm super grateful he paid homage to all of us, and if Bruno and I ever get to meet, I just want to tell him here, "I appreciate that."

Being blessed with the Soul Train Music Legend Award in 2016 was equally thrilling, and what a night that was! It was so much fun from beginning to end, from walking in on the red carpet with all my children to standing up on stage and thanking them with a speech that was not the one I had written, but one I just winged in the moment. I told myself before I went up, "The most important names to remember to thank are your mother, God, and your children."

The joy of it was infectious for all of us, especially when I went from that podium out onto the live stage to perform for them and the rest of the arena cheering us on, celebrating those hits and all the artists like Doug E. Fresh, V. Bozeman, Wreckx-n-Effect, Bobby Brown, and Guy, who came out to perform with me. I didn't just want to let the award do the talking that night, but to blow the whole crowd and the watching world away with the hottest live performance of the night.

The *only* downside was Chauncey Hannibal's refusal to perform our signature Blackstreet hit "No Diggity" with me and the band. And after all I've done for him throughout his career? He was the one downside of that otherwise glorious night, especially the reunion between Aaron Hall and me, both musically and personally.

After that night, Aaron and I realized the fans missed us, and in 2017 we reunited Guy for a Legends Tour that took us all over the country, playing before sold-out crowds who still knew our songs word for word and could sing and scream them with the same energy they'd had at our shows twenty years earlier. We'd all grown up together and stayed friends through the music, and I can't even describe how great it felt to be on stage with Aaron and Damion again, listening to the classic blend of our trio coming out of the monitors night after night. It was truly musical magic that only the three of us can make.

CHAPTER NINETEEN

6405 Hollywood Boulevard

*"Riley's illustrious catalogue encompasses
a massive list of timeless hits."*

—HOLLYWOOD WALK OF FAME INDUCTION COMMITTEE

Given how many number one love songs I've written, I've often been asked over the years about what a lady can expect on a date with Teddy Riley. I've never tried to impress a woman as much as show the gentleman in me, so of course, we do dinner and the horse-and-carriage ride. I took my current fiancée to my nephew's wedding for our first date, and it just so happened my mother was there, so she could meet my mother and the rest of my family. We've been together a couple of years now.

She's a singer and a songwriter, so it was basically a match made in heaven. We write songs together and have a synergy, and that's what I've been searching for, that synergy. Confessionally, with the relationship I'm in now, I had to learn how to trust, learn how to communicate and adjust, but at the same time, I never want to think negatively, because I'm a creative person. Creative people don't like to think outside of the realm of creation, so if the relationship is not creative, then that can spell disaster.

Now, it's okay to have differences, disagreements, and even debates when that creates the song, because when you're mad at your spouse, something is coming out in a song. That sort of emotional and sexual tension gave me many of my biggest hits back in the day.

Some of the best songs can come from potential breakups. After an argument or not speaking to your partner for a while, you might wind up writing a song about it. In my first relationship, my partner had commitment issues, and I would see her with other guys. I don't ever want to wonder about these things; I don't want anything to throw me off the creative flow that I have every day. A lot of times that's why my relationships didn't work, because I was at my most creative and not so much into taking care of the relationship. After all, the music is my bread and butter. The relationship doesn't make me anything.

Let me take you through some songs that I created from my relationships, and some I created from those of other people. "Let's Chill," for instance, was basically written by myself with Aaron Hall and Bernard Belle, but I did all the music, and it was inspired by my relationship with Donna Deguzman, the mother of my four oldest children. We were on the verge of breaking up, and one day I just said, "I want to make a song that will basically answer the question of whether we're going to be together for the rest of our lives." It was the conversation piece that made her stay.

I wrote "Remember the Time," "Joy," and "Let's Stay Together" when Donna and I were again on the verge of breaking up. I write songs that help me with my relationships because it's how I communicate. We were on the outs because of me and the things I'd done, cheating, which made me write those songs for her, and they really brought us together and took us through almost sixteen years. Those were the songs that helped us make it last. Then you have those songs like "Rump Shaker," "Booti Call," and "I Wanna." Those are inspired by *different* kinds of relationships.

◆ ◆ ◆ ◆ ◆

I experienced yet another full-circle moment professionally in 2018 when I came home to Harlem, where it all started for me, to receive the Key to the City. The city officials had declared an official "New Jack City Day." It is hard to put into words how I felt given that it was on those very streets that I first formed the sound. The Apollo Theater rolled out the red carpet, with an all-star lineup that had gathered to help celebrate me receiving my key to Harlem along with Keith Sweat, Damion Hall, and Kool Moe Dee.

The New York State Legislature recognized us as well that day, with a very impressive lineup of political power that showed up to be part of the party and make it official, including New York State Senator Brian Benjamin, Assemblywoman Inez Dickens, U.S. Congressman Adriano Espaillat, City Councilman Bill Perkins, Manhattan Borough President Gale Brewer, Mayor Bill de Blasio, and even HRH Queen Diambi Kabatusuila of the Democratic Republic of Congo.

Apollo Theater executive Kamilah Forbes gave a wonderful address that day about my career and its place in Harlem musical history, recalling that "for eighty-five years, the Apollo Theater has been a space for Black excellence and American cultural innovation, and every day we strive to celebrate the contributions that African American artists have made on global popular culture. So it is fitting that we take a minute to mark thirty years of the enormous impact of New Jack Swing and celebrate Harlem's own Mr. Teddy Riley, the architect behind the New Jack Swing sound."

To top the homecoming off, the legendary Harlem Globetrotters asked me to write and produce a new, updated theme song for them. Of course I jumped at the opportunity, and what an amazing connection to have, especially since I'd grown up a big fan of the team. It's an incredible feeling to get to work with an institution like that, which I'd watched since my childhood.

In fact, every day at 3 p.m. when school let out, I used to run home to watch the animated Globetrotters show, which had as big an influence on my life as watching The Jackson 5's cartoon. For the new, updated theme, I put a beat behind it that came to me from the actual style and history of the Globetrotters; it felt like jazz, and it's in a major chord, so I had to do something that would be different but that people would still recognize is true to the Globetrotters' legacy.

◆ ◆ ◆ ◆ ◆

As great as the love from the East Coast was, every musician, no matter where they come from, will find themselves dreaming of having their very own star on the Hollywood Walk of Fame. Whether you're a TV, movie, or music star, this is the ultimate acknowledgment of having left a permanent footprint on the entertainment business. In 2019, the call finally came that it was my turn to put my hands in the cement. I couldn't believe it; I felt like a little kid running around my house, looking for my mom to tell her the big news. She was the first person I told and first person I thanked at the ceremony, because I feel that, above anyone else, she definitely deserved to share that moment and award with me.

She sat in the front, as always, but didn't know I was going to thank her as early in my acceptance speech as I did, so she stood up, waved, and then sat back down. I had to give her flowers, because many of us don't have our parents to give flowers to. That's the one thing with my mother: I never wanted her to miss any moment that I celebrated. I wanted her to get the accolades for everything.

My mother and God get the credit, because he blessed me with the talent, and she saw that and let me set up my first recording studio in her apartment in the Harlem projects. So traveling all the way across the country and standing on the Walk of Fame on Hollywood Boulevard about to be given my very own star, that was a moment we had to share together, because it belonged to her too.

That was an amazing feeling, and consistent with my goal throughout my career of just continuing to make my mother proud. My children were all there, too, which was very cool because they got to see what Dad had worked so hard for over the years. What that star on the Hollywood Walk of Fame meant to me was that I'd made it: I made it and if I quit today, there's a star with my name on it that will shine forever.

Proudly, the Rileys are a close family, and just as much as I love showing up to my children's ball games or dance recitals as they grow up, I love it when they are all together for special moments like holidays or coming with Dad to the Soul Train Awards and the Hollywood Walk of Fame. I was definitely Coolest Dad of the Day with their friends for those twenty-four hours.

After my mother, there were several VIP folks behind the scenes who were instrumental in making that honor happen, beginning with Yvonne McNair, who I want to make sure I thank again in print. She did what a manager is supposed to do, and got my name formally submitted to the committee that decides who is awarded stars.

I want to make sure I also thank the one and only LL Cool J, who officially voted me in. I feel like I owe him extra thanks because he didn't have to do that. I commend his heart, because relationships in the music business can cut both ways. Some stars feel like every one of their peers are the competition, but LL was from New York and had, I think, heard and seen the reverberations of my sound through the last thirty years of hip-hop and felt it was time.

The Hollywood Walk of Fame released their own official statement declaring, "The Hollywood Chamber of Commerce has honored recording artist/music producer Teddy Riley with the 2,670th Star on the World Famous Hollywood Walk of Fame, in the Category of Recording, on August 16, 2019, in Los Angeles. The star has been dedicated in the category of Recording at 6405 Hollywood Boulevard. For more than 30 years, Grammy Award–winning, multiplatinum music icon Teddy Riley has embodied the spirit of innovation and ingenuity as a recording artist, songwriter, producer, composer, arranger, engineer, and all-around trailblazer. With more than 1,000 credits to his name, the legendary Riley has amassed a host of awards and accolades throughout his storied career for his incredibly vast contributions to music, which include being credited as the creator of New Jack Swing, the groundbreaking genre that redefined the musical landscape of the 1980s and '90s."

It's strange how Hollywood works, and the record business in general, because the day of the ceremony, I saw people I hadn't seen in *years*. In some cases, it was a simple matter of them living out in California and me in Virginia Beach or Atlanta without our paths crossing again. That they came out to show me love was welcome, though tough in some cases. I played the game and smiled for the cameras, but was thinking, *You haven't spoken to me in so long. Why appear all of a sudden?* That didn't just extend to certain individuals, but to the corporate vultures that can come circling when they see an opportunity to make money off you.

This being such a roller-coaster business by nature, it was quite something to watch how the media hype over the star actually made me "hot" again in the eyes of certain legacy agencies in Hollywood like United Talent Agency. One of the biggest in the game, they came knocking at my door, eager to sign me after the unveiling of my star. I was of course happy to sign, given the whole song and dance they sold me to get me on their roster, but I was reminded quickly enough—once again—of what a political business this is.

The politics of the entertainment business can really suck, as you're dealing in some cases with the biggest manipulators—operators who are ultimately for the star who's shining brightest right now, versus those with the longevity. So once I saw I wasn't truly a priority for UTA, I left that deal because of the bullshit, plain and simple. They were doing money signings, not longevity signings.

Luckily for me, I had not just a legacy but an active fan base that I'd worked very hard to build in the first place, and that had grown by then into an extended family. That meant I not only would see the couples I'd known since they were dating back in the Guy heyday of the early 1990s, through Blackstreet shows when their kids were young, to shows throughout the 2000s when those kids were teenagers, but also to the 2010s, when I started seeing their grandkids. I had watched three generations of families growing up coming to see my shows.

I know they could have spent that time and money on anything, so it has always meant the world to me that my fans have stuck by me through thick and thin with such loyalty and love. I know many of them by their first names, along with their children. I love the idea that maybe I'm inspiring one or two of those kids to follow in my footsteps, either on the stage or in the studio, or wherever they want to go in life. I hope my music has been an inspiration and the soundtrack to at least a favorite memory or two, because all of you have given me a million of my own.

CHAPTER TWENTY

Verzuz— Teddy Riley and Kenny "Babyface" Edmonds

"Originally, I wasn't going to do Verzuz. I didn't like the idea of competing, I didn't like that at all. Frankly, I thought with Teddy's catalog, 'I don't want to go up against him!' That's when Andre Harrell got involved, and had texted me in a group text and ultimately he convinced me. He explained, 'This is not a competition, it's just a celebration of music . . .' Once he got to the game, Teddy Riley inspired me to want to keep going and push harder and win. Nobody did it like he did it, and I felt like he was responsible for that whole era with New Jack Swing.

*He likes to be at the top of the game, and whenever he's
there, he's not going to accept anything less than being
number one. He's a very talented guy and remains so, and
someone I feel who has not just changed the face of music
to a certain extent, but who has also inspired me. What
Verzuz did was shine a light on both of us and both of
our careers, and earned us the title of the G.O.A.T.S."*
—KENNY "BABYFACE" EDMONDS, SINGER,
SONGWRITER, AND PRODUCER

The creation of Verzuz was one of those inspired moments of
invention during the COVID-19 lockdown that showed the
true power music has to uplift and bring people together from all
walks of life, especially during a dark time like the one we were all
sharing. With millions of music fans stuck at home, glued to their
laptops and smartphones as their only link to the outside world,
some musicians were moved to innovate in order to keep their product out there and revenue coming in while they couldn't tour. Timbaland and Swizz Beatz had a stroke of genius that struck like
lightning and electrified cyberspace.

The Verzuz concept was brilliant in its simplicity: Two superstar
producers face off over Zoom, from their respective lockdown studios, in a friendly competition, a duel playing their biggest hits back
and forth live while fans tune in. Timbaland's popularity with millennials who had grown up dreaming of being in the music business

and watching *Empire* was already secure enough that when word went out to his Instagram followers to tune in for the very first battle between Timbaland and Swizz, thousands of people logged on.

Drawing the kind of views that any artist, band, or producer would dream of, that inaugural face-off brought in over a million viewers, and the first Instagram Live music competition show took off: Boi-1da vs. Hit-Boy, The-Dream vs. Sean Garrett, Ne-Yo vs. Johntá Austin, Scott Storch vs. Mannie Fresh, Ryan Tedder vs. Benny Blanco, T-Pain vs. Lil Jon, and RZA vs. DJ Premier. Virtual viewing parties began happening all over the world as Verzuz caught fire across social and music media. Slots were filling up fast, but "Dream Team-Ups" were continually being floated on social media by the fans, which in a way I felt was the most organic kind of invitation to get.

The inevitable showdown, Babyface vs. Teddy Riley, was beginning to catch a buzz, from Instagram to Twitter and Facebook. Soon enough, Babyface's and my phones began blowing up, not from social media alerts but from veteran music executives like Andre Harrell, who thought such a face-off would be huge. He argued this would not only be great for the fans but for both of us, too, in terms of introducing our respective catalogs to a new teenage fan base of potential listeners.

Initially, I wasn't very hot on the idea and Babyface (who I call Kenny) wasn't either. We'd known each other for decades by then and remained friends, with a healthy respect for the styles, songs, and sounds we'd both invented and dominated radio with over the same era. In a friendly way, Kenny and I had been competing on the charts for years, and we each had our initial reasons for feeling reluctant to compete in this new arena, including not wanting to be viewed as explicit rivals.

It turned out Andre Harrell was having the same sort of conversations behind the scenes with both Kenny and me. Andre, being the visionary he always has been, saw this as an opportunity and wound up talking both of us into it with this pitch: "Do it for the culture. It's not a competition. It's just to celebrate you guys." When he put it to me like that, it sunk in, and I said, "I got it! Let's go!" The way I'd initially left it with Andre was simple: "If Babyface is in, I am."

After Andre hit me back saying Kenny was in, I finally started to get excited about it. Then to hype it up, we took a boxing poster from some Tyson fight and Photoshopped Kenny's face on top of the boxer who was wearing a robe, and then Photoshopped mine on top of a photo of Mike Tyson wearing a fur. We kept doing promotional bits to make it look like it was a real thing. All the while, my respect level for Babyface was on ten. Initially, I felt like I couldn't be in a room with a guy I'd looked up to for a long time, since the beginning of my career. When I discovered Kenny, I discovered my big brother.

I'd watched a few of the live-stream battles before ours, both to wrap my head around the concept and to look for an edge that I thought might make our face-off just a little hotter than the competition of producer versus producer. The answer came to me in an epiphany: I wouldn't just show up with my biggest hits, but with a real live band to play them instead of it just being through the computer, console, or turntables. The best part of the surprise is it wasn't only going to be one for viewers, but for Babyface too. I not only brought the full band but also set up our full live production in my house, complete with PA, live backup singers, and my amazing band of instruments. We were ready to blow the roof off.

Unfortunately, when the big night arrived, we found ourselves mired in technical glitches on Instagram's end that made it an absolute catastrophe for viewers. From the Zoom feeds buffering at different points, which caused delays in one of our songs' starting in response to the other's finishing, to audio issues, it was embarrassing all around and made both of us sound and look awful in front of a million-plus viewing audience. But contrary to the news stories that started swirling around shortly thereafter, I have the actual true performance with no feedback and, in spite of the glitches, it was flawless.

I thought it was all going to go smoothly because we'd just had a concert three weeks before with Blackstreet, and I used the exact same production, and it all worked out perfectly. Fans out there need to know that I kept playing because I had no idea Instagram was having all these technical glitches. That first night was all on Instagram. Everybody has acknowledged it wasn't my fault, but unfortunately, when I played back the first night, that's how it looked: like I had messed up. Our competition was too much for their servers.

That performance kicked off a social media buzz that today I call "The Overnight Success," because even though the memes were all on me and a little bit on Babyface, within twenty-four hours, 782,000 people had clicked onto us streaming. Talk of a rematch started getting hyped all over social media. People didn't know at first that there was even going to be a rematch, but once the first night aired, everybody was calling—I think even *clamoring*—for one. It was almost like everybody went to buy their tickets, even though there weren't any tickets. We had over four million impressions as people watched that rematch, and today, it's still one of the most watched of those Verzuz competitions; no one has gotten bigger numbers than we did, not even Snoop Dogg, and I thought for sure Snoop would beat us out.

This was new technology being tested in front of the whole world with us as the lab rats—and that's not a position even the bravest of artists would normally volunteer to be in once, let alone twice. The real-time surrealistic truth of the whole thing was almost impossible to describe. It was a bona fide shit show that on any other day would have been annihilated in the press but was spun as though it was a warm-up match for the headlining battle still to come. That only hyped up talk of a rematch even more, even as neither of us was initially very interested in a repeat. It wound up taking more mediating from Andre, who emphasized the opportunity this was for both of us if we could see past the technical issues to the big picture. Andre has since passed away, but he remains a great mentor whose advice I've followed since the beginning of my career, and I'm sure glad Kenny and I both listened to it one more time, for the sake of what was to come.

As *People* magazine reported amid the frenzy over our first attempted showdown, "The highly anticipated Instagram Live battle between legendary music producers Kenny 'Babyface' Edmonds and Teddy Riley was brought to a halt by technical issues Saturday night, forcing them to postpone their duel. With more than 400,000 viewers tuned in to watch the live stream take place on Saturday night, audio issues, specifically on Riley's end, derailed the face-off between the two. During the live broadcast, Babyface, 62, was ready to go and seen sitting in a studio, while Riley, 52, appeared to prepare more for a concert with a setup that led to echoing and playback every time he tried to play a song. After about an hour of troubleshooting, Babyface concluded that they would make another attempt at their friendly competition at another time. In the aftermath of the failed battle, social media users took to various platforms to drag the two R&B producers, with many poking fun at their ages and the inability to use Instagram. Even celebrities joined in on the good fun, including Adele, Mariah Carey, Snoop Dogg, Diddy and Toni Braxton . . . The showdown between Babyface and Riley was the most watched battle yet."

Ahead of our second face-off, Babyface and I didn't speak. But the *first* thing I had my people do was communicate with Swizz Beatz's folks and the technical people at Instagram to make sure there weren't going to be any repeats of the glitches. On the one hand, it had been an ironic blessing because it had raised so much hype, but on the other, if I didn't pull off a victory that second night, all anyone would ever talk about was the first. I'd been a performer my whole life, but this was going to be a first performance of its kind for me, online before an audience of not just thousands but *millions*, old fans as well as the new generation that was just preparing to tune in for the first time.

I was nervous heading into the ring that night, too, let me tell you. I was saying to myself, "You've got a second chance—you better not mess this one up!" So, what I did was I prayed and called Breon, a close friend of mine, who gave me confidence that all would go well. I was such a fan of Kenny's whole catalog, and though I'd gotten a preview of what he might throw at me from the first night, I was expecting him to mix it up now that he'd gotten into the spirit of the competition. I even got Dr. Dre on the phone while the Verzuz competition was live streaming.

TMZ got in on the act, as this had become such a hot word-on-the-street type of story, reporting amid the rematch that "the two R&B icons hopped back on the 'Gram Monday night to pick up where they left off over the weekend. Teddy and Face were on the same page . . . and did exactly what artists are supposed to do for these Live battles—namely, play their biggest hits back and forth, and let the audience tuning in to decide who takes the round. That went on for a solid hour."

Fortunately, we both walked away victorious on the second night, after dazzling the generations of fans watching and listening. We kept hitting them with hit after hit, whether it was Babyface with "Don't Be Cruel" or me with "My Prerogative." It was a draw by the time we were done because anyone could see how inspired we both were in that moment. It proved we were the G.O.A.T.s of Verzuz and the R&B business. My Instagram went from 150,000 to a million followers overnight.

We'd both been in the business over forty years by that point, and understood it was a young man's game by nature. We were grateful to be competing with their numbers on social media. Beyond that, it turned out we had a few fans in the media, too, like the folks over at CNN and Trevor Noah on *The Daily Show*, who had us both on the next day and had such kind words for us both, making the important point that "we're trying to find ways to connect. We're trying to find ways to create a semblance of normal life. You broke Instagram in a way that it had never been broken before, having a Verzuz battle. You've essentially imbued yourselves through multiple generations of cultures. I wonder if you yourselves were shocked to see not just how many people were consuming what you were doing, but the vast range of people that had been influenced by what you've created throughout your lives . . . The range, it spanned across time. Teddy, when I was watching you, there were truly moments of joy on your face when Babyface would play a song, and then there were moments of joy on his face when you would play a song. It was the feeling we were all experiencing when watching this Instagram Live, it was a feeling of love. I honestly hope you appreciate what you did for everybody; it was one of the most amazing experiences that I think a group of people have had together on the internet for a really long time."

After that appearance, word was *out*. So many journalists from so many different television shows, podcasts, and print and online publications wanted to have us on their programs to talk about our showdown. *Variety* even called us up, which actually made me take a step back, because it was like, *Wait a minute, this is really big!* Then, as the numbers started to come in on competitive streaming content that had aired the same time as our rematch, we found out that we had beaten out former First Lady Michelle Obama. It was just the kind of phenomenal moment I'd enjoyed during previous eras of my career, but to see both Babyface and me receiving that kind of front-page, headline-grabbing love and acknowledgment felt like another level of appreciation altogether.

I'm going to put it out there like this and be transparent: My show helped make Verzuz what it is today, performance-wise. They were doing it very cheesily. The production was small. But when I did what I did, because "Teddy Doing Too Much" is my nickname, it set a precedent. They have to do too much now because I raised the bar both creatively and commercially. Adding Apple Music as a plat-form, the show would use that momentum to rocket into a success-ful season the following fall, with new face-offs between Brandy and Monica, Ashanti and Keyshia Cole, who brought in over six million views, and Jeezy and Gucci Mane, who brought in five million. The numbers kept climbing as we made musical history.

CHAPTER TWENTY-ONE

Forgiveness

Even after everything that happened with Gene Griffin, years later in 2005, someone from his family reached out and said that Gene wanted to talk to me. It turned out that Gene was in the early stages of Alzheimer's. I told this emissary that I could never forget what Gene had done to me, but that I could forgive him, because at one point, he had been like a father to me, keeping me secluded from some of the worst aspects of the business. If he hadn't, I'd have been doing drugs and conforming to other industry standards of back in the day. But I didn't smoke, I didn't drink, I didn't party. Gene kept me away from all that.

They brought him to Virginia, where I was living, and I immediately felt like I was seeing my father again, because my real father was barely in my life when I was growing up. Without all the other people around, this is when I realized God had put us back together because he was sick. He was near the end at that point, and I was one of the only people he still remembered. His nephew was in the car with him because Gene had started falling asleep on the road driving back and forth from Atlanta to DC to see his wife. He showed up at my brother's house, and then I took him to see my daughter, Deja, who was still young. Gene said, "That's my goddaughter, man, she growin' up," and kept repeating it like he'd never said it.

At first, I thought he was just getting older, because I didn't yet know what Alzheimer's was. But I felt like, if he was gonna go, I wanted to be part of his joy, so from that day forth, we kept seeing each other when he went back and forth to DC, and the beauty of it all was I just embraced him even more every day I saw him, because it was like seeing my father again. I finally saw my godmother, Maram Griffin, too. We kept visiting more regularly from that point, until one day I stopped hearing from them altogether.

Then, out of the blue, after some time had passed, I got a call from a highway patrolman asking if I knew Gene Griffin.

I said, "Yes, I do. What is wrong?"

The officer told me Gene and his nephew were driving to DC and had stopped at a gas station. When his nephew went in to pay for the gas, Gene forgot he was in the store and drove off without him. He left his nephew in South Carolina and was found later in North Carolina, outside Charlotte, asleep in his car.

When the police knocked on the window and woke Gene up, they asked, "Sir, do you know where you're at? Do you have a nephew?" because his nephew had called 911 and they'd put an APB out for Gene.

When they asked him about his nephew's whereabouts, he said, "Yeah, sure, he's in the store," and then they told him, "You left your nephew back in South Carolina." They reached out to me initially because my name was the first one they found in his phone book and he asked them to call me.

Once it was all straightened out and he was on his way back to Atlanta with his nephew, it really sunk in for me that Gene's mind was fading fast, and that realization took a toll on me. I started reading up on Alzheimer's and learned that eventually your mind erases your memories of everyone and everything. A sense of urgency came over me and the next day, I got in my car and headed down to Georgia to see him, fearing this might be one of the last times Gene would remember me.

When I arrived, I stayed and visited with him for a while, and then asked the staff at the facility he was living in if they would help me take him out to the rehearsal for a concert I was performing in Atlanta that night. Beyond that, I asked them, "Please get him out of here as much as you can, because mentally there's nothing in here to make him remember." At one point during the rehearsal, I stopped and jumped into a Guy song, just so I could be a part of bringing Gene's memory back one more time.

After the song was done, I hopped off stage, went up to him, and asked, "You remember that?"

He replied, "Yeah man, yeah, I remember," and I said, "That was the time! We had a great time doing that music."

He was remembering! "I know, man, I remember that. That was the time."

Then I asked, "You wanna come out on the road with me?"

Gene got very excited and said, "Yeah, man, you just let me know when. I'll go, no problem."

After that, we had some more rehearsals in Atlanta and then a studio session, and the night I went in to work at Icon Studios, my assistant came in and told me I had a phone call. I went out to answer, and his people told me, "We lost him. We lost Gene." I broke down. Then I got on the phone with his wife to figure out the funeral. I stayed in Atlanta to make sure everything ran smoothly, and I went to the memorial and even spoke at the funeral. I told everyone how much of a father Gene was to me, and I felt very at peace.

BLKRC and the 2020s

"Riley, a Grammy-winning, multiplatinum producer, is credited with creating New Jack Swing, a fusion genre of music incorporating contemporary R&B, hip-hop, gospel, soul and pop . . . with over 1,000 credits to his name."

—VARIETY, 2024

I t amuses me sometimes when I think that I have never won the Producer of the Year Grammy, though people generally consider me to be one of the most influential producers of all time. I didn't get some awards because I'm not "in." There are different projects I didn't get hired on throughout my career because I wasn't willing to play the game of living in LA and constantly networking at industry events, hustling for new work. That's why I've consistently had to invent my own trends. The reality of being a record producer with a long-term career is that there are times when everybody is coming to you, which was my reality in the wake of New Jack Swing's explosion through Bobby Brown, Keith Sweat, and Guy. Sometimes I had to shut my phone off in order to get any music done.

Then after Michael Jackson's success, that became a global chorus—from the K-Pop crowd to Snoop Dogg. But those opportunities came to me. I didn't seek them out. Ironically, though I've generated hundreds of millions of dollars based on my music throughout my forty-year career, I have probably suffered financially in my career because that particular scorecard hasn't interested me. What keeps me excited, if I'm not working with legends like Snoop and MJ, is working with new talent, whether developing it on my own, as with Blackstreet, or with the new artists I have developed from the ground floor to the top of the charts.

I have prevailed and stayed relevant throughout my career by always inventing my own original music, original acts, original hits, and original sound. That's why I'm still doing what I love today for a living, and it's taken me and my sound all over the world: to Korea, to Japan, to Africa. I'll be honest: The first time I traveled to Africa, I was afraid to go. The specific country was Nigeria, and people kept telling me I was going to need security because of the threat stars there face of being kidnapped for money. Sure enough, I had five or six bodyguards with me every minute, everywhere I went, but the local people were wonderfully friendly to me. I was performing at the Eko Hotel, where I had the honor of meeting some of the best

DJs in the country. After that trip, I now have people I consider family in Nigeria, like Mancooli and Chiamba, movers and shakers and go-getters over there, and also humanitarians, because they give back. If I need anything, they're always there for me, and now Nigeria is one of my favorite places to go.

I've shared the stage with artists like Sadikki and Fally Ipupa, who is widely regarded as one of the top Congolese musicians in the world, and Mohambi, who is one of the most profound songwriters I've ever worked with. I've been to Senegal, Rwanda, Congo, Cape Verde, Morocco, Guinea—across the entire African continent, and not only watched men and women who had grown up on New Jack Swing and Michael Jackson singing my songs back to me when I performed them, but also equally as many children doing so whenever we gave concerts in schools. One that stands out was in Rwanda, where I performed "No Diggity" at a school with kids who ranged from elementary school all the way to high school. And what a talented group! Their harmonies and performance were amazing, and though English wasn't their first language, they knew *every word* of that song. That just trips me out now to even think about it. I have been blessed through my songs to make a truly universal musical connection with listeners all over the world.

◆ ◆ ◆ ◆ ◆

Everyone was doing their best to make me feel at home everywhere I traveled in Africa, including on my third trip, when I visited Senegal. I stayed at the most incredible hotel in Dakar called The Palms, which I thought was affiliated with the chain. This wasn't a five-star hotel, this was a ten-star. The owners are like my sisters. They originally came from America, moved to Senegal, and now run this hotel, and I owe them both a profound thank you for making me feel so welcome—and equally, for making me feel even more comfortable with Africa. I feel like God, just as He always has, is navigating for me these days, leading me to inspiring new places and people. On that trip, I went from Senegal to Guinea, then Lisbon, and ultimately to Cape Verde. I fell in love with the place and its peacefulness, with being able to walk outside and not be mobbed by everyone. And this being the digital age, I was still able to make music while I was overseas, working over Zoom with groups all over the world, from some of those African artists to others back in the U.S.

One of the greatest gifts music has given me throughout my life is the new places it's taken me, and in 2024, I found myself sitting down with some of the world's top educators, who were interested in developing master classes in New Jack Swing. I was immediately on board, and we've been working hard developing a curriculum that will be taught in classrooms everywhere around the globe. I feel like New Jack Swing is a sound and musical style that belongs to the world. As its most expert professor, so to speak, I look forward to deconstructing its creation, evolution, and history for new generations of young minds who are interested in the genre.

Meanwhile, I try to grow every day, to keep putting the best of myself, personally and creatively, into the life I live. As I approach sixty, I'm blessed that I can enjoy the fruits of my labor. Money doesn't really motivate me anymore the way it did when I had nine children to raise and put through college, and also had other family members to support. I'm proud that when I was still a teenager, I moved my entire family out of the Harlem projects, and that my children grew up with luxuries I couldn't have dreamed of as a kid. Today, I'm proud to watch as my children have and continue to grow into adults, beaming in their own light. They've all stepped out of their dad's shadow and are making their own mark in the world.

When it comes to performing live, I have decided that I will now headline as Teddy Riley only. I toured off and on throughout the 2010s with Guy, and I've talked enough about the drama that makes that experience no longer enjoyable for me. At my age, I'm happier with the peace I have doing a solo show, and after coheadlining a tour with New Edition in 2023, I realized I had enough loyalty from my fans to carry on as a solo artist.

To keep it 100 percent real, I made more playing on my own than the entire group got paid on our previous Guy tour, and now I didn't have to divide the money up three ways. Better yet, I was able to do my show my way with my band—and have a much better time with my fans. Believe it or not, people can actually feel the tension within a group, and they felt the tension when it came to Guy and the old Blackstreet, the combustibility of the chemistry, and that's not healthy for anyone coming to relax and blow off steam at what is supposed to be a carefree concert on a Friday night.

People don't always realize it, but when band members stay together for decades touring, it's not always because they love spending time together. Often, off stage, they have separate dressing rooms and separate tour buses to keep the peace. That all costs a fortune. It's ridiculous to cater to that sort of ego when, as professionals, our job is to go out and perform for the crowd. They're the stars of the show, not us. That's how I've always looked at it. I'm not taking away from Aaron Hall's talent as a lead vocalist or live performer, but over the years, whenever we fought about money or whatever other past issues might have still been lingering, it distracted from the show we needed to be focused on.

I remember a friend telling me about being at my backstage birthday party in Atlanta and seeing a group of fans surrounding me asking for autographs while Aaron just stood alone off in a corner, staring at me with a stone face. I know that jealousy because it exists in every group, but usually it's when the performers are young and fighting for the spotlight. Here, Aaron and I shared it on stage equally, and I'm sure that the fans were moving over to him next. But we weren't signing those autographs and taking those selfies together, and maybe because I've worked with Michael Jackson or because I'm known as the producer who invented the genre Guy flourished in, I attracted a bit more in the way of fan attention than he did that night. I don't see Guy from that vantage point, but heading into the 2020s, I finally decided that I needed to cut that bad karma loose once and for all. I have always had a saying: "Miss me with the bullshit," which means there's no room for that on a stage at the level I play at.

So from here on, I will be performing as the Teddy Riley Experience, playing all my hits and bringing out a new super-group, BLKRC, to back me up. They're like Earth, Wind & Fire meets Arrested Development and are very diverse: I have an African singer, a Latina singer, an Italian Michael Bolton, and my country singer, who is the country Heavy D. Meanwhile, I'm doing songs in the studio with Jelly Roll, Teddy Swims, and Gregory Porter. I want to create a spectacularly diverse album, and then bring the entire project to the stage with a multipiece orchestra.

In concert, I can't do anything small unless it's an impromptu jam session, because my fans expect me to bring them the night of their lives. The adrenaline you feel when you're live on stage, sharing that energy and synergy with the crowd, is incredible. The connection feels electric. At the same time, I get such a warmhearted feeling when I see people singing my songs back to me.

When people are willing, especially with inflation and the high price of basics like food and gasoline these days, to spend their hard-earned money to come see me play a show, it's never lost on me how much of a privilege that is for me. To have the opportunity to share my music with you decade after decade, where I've seen many of those same faces as teenagers, then adults, then as members of their own new families—that is indescribable. I see six-year-olds dancing out there, and it reminds me of being that same age at the Apollo, dancing away to Gladys Knight. Who knows? Maybe one day, one of those kids dancing and singing along to New Jack Swing will be the next Teddy Riley.

ACKNOWLEDGMENTS

The Most High, God; my mom and Dad: Mildred Riley aka Momma Riley, Edward Junior Riley; my brother, Markell Riley; and my sister, Joyce Nese Riley . . . RIP.

My family: Deja Riley, Taja Riley, Bobbie Riley, Nia Riley, TJ Riley, Teddy Riley II, Samar Riley, Mykal Riley, Sokari Riley; my grandchildren: Kameryn Lavender, Babyboy Sage Izydorczyk aka Baby Riley; Auntie Liz Riley and Patrick Riley.

The mothers of my children: Donna Roberts, Madeline Nelson, Nicole Greene, Lateasha Deguzman! My better half, Cynthia "Sky Monroe" Pareja, and stepson, Zavien.

Uncs/father figures: Uncle Willie Brewington, Sam Douglas, Robert Gusto Wells, Gene Griffin, Unc Mike Concepcion, Royal Bayyan, Benjamin Wright, Gerald Albright, Edwin Birdsong (RIP). Thank you all for keeping me focused on my craft.

My extended family: Babysitters . . . twins Karen and Sharon from 240, Denise Barrow, Wayne Barrow, Mom Burke, Fabian and Tara Chandler, Ty Fyffe, and Lyle Mann.

My friends/brotherhood: Flavor Flav; ProHoeZak, Virgil, Bernard

"Coach" Alexander, Greg Walker, Prinston Moon, Chris Gremlin, AP, Sir, Randy.

My IT team and studio arch/builder: Quincy Boston and Will Warlwyn.

My group: J-Stylz, Rodney Poe, LJ from Profile (now BLKRC), and my musicians!

My Virginia family, New York family, ATL family, and Vegas family.

Past and present partners/business mates: Jimmy Iovine; Clarence Avant, Clive Calder, Simon & Schuster, Ricky Husky.

CFO: Juanita "Twin" Brown, the Queen of Trading!

Accountant: Thomas Smith

Assistants: Rashaad Donelson and Anthony Bynum

Photographer: Marc Baptiste

My co-writer, Jake Brown, for working on the book with me, and our agent, Frank Weimann, for finding a great publisher.

Tony Thompson, Johnny Kemp, the great Michael Jackson for having me as a part of his journey! Rest in paradise!

—Teddy Riley

I'd first and foremost like to thank Teddy Riley for the incredible opportunity over the past decade to get to know you and help tell your one-of-a-kind story; my amazing agent, Frank Weimann, and the entire staff at Folio Literary Management for your belief, counsel, representation, and help bringing this project to Charles Suitt at 13A Books/Gallery Books/Simon & Schuster, and our amazing editor, Aimée Bell, and Hanna Preston and Sierra Fang-Horvath; our amazing cast of contributors who gave their time to interviewing for the project, from Kool Moe Dee to Big Daddy Kane, Mildred Riley, Markell Riley, Bobby Brown, Kenny "Babyface" Edmonds, the late, great Andre Harrell, Pharrell Williams, Rodney Jerkins, Keith Sweat, Tara Thomas, Darren Hastings, Daryl Jones, Barry Michael Cooper for the amazing foreword, and more; *Rolling Stone* magazine for the wonderful prerelease coverage; my wife, Carrie Brock-Brown, and our Westie, Molly; my parents, James and Tina-Thieme Brown, for letting me listen to Teddy Riley records growing up in the '80s from age ten onward; my brother, Ret. Sgt. Joshua Timothy Brown, Jenna Brown, and my nephew, Greyson Liam Brown; my in-laws, Bill and Susan Brock, and little Gizmo; my beloved grandmother, Jacquelyn Thieme; the Thieme, Brown, and Schweiss families; my extended family of friends, Alex Schuchard, Cris Ellauri, Andrew McDermott, Sean Fillinich, Bob O'Brien, Richard Kendrick, and Alexandra Federov; my *About the Authors TV* collaborators, Ray Riddle, Allan McCall, and Premiere Pete; Ed Seimann, Tiffany Baile, and everyone at MVD; my irreplaceable assistant, Elvia Schroeder; Edward McDonald for the opportunity to help tell your story; Aaron Harmon for taking a musical journey with me in the studio the past two decades; Tony and Yvonne Rose; Joe Satriani; Ann and Nancy Wilson; Lemmy Kilmister; Afeni Shakur and Dina LaPolt; Joe Viers; and anyone else who has been a part of my creative corner the past twenty-five years.

—**Jake Brown**